# Orphan Girl

*The Memoir of a Chicago Bag Lady*

# MARIE JAMES
*as told to*
Jane Hertenstein

Cornerstone Press Chicago
CHICAGO, ILLINOIS

This is a memoir; as such, it contains perceptions of life and incidents
from the teller's perspective. Names have been changed in the story to
protect the privacy of those still living.

Published by
Cornerstone Press Chicago
939 W. Wilson Ave.
Chicago, IL 60640
*cspress@jpusa.chi.il.us*

Printed in the United States of America
*Cover and interior design and layout by Pat Peterson/wheatsdesign*
*Cover illustration by Janet Cameron*
*Photography by Terrence Wheeler*

02 01 00 99 98 5 4 3 2 1

Library of Congress Cataloging-in-Publication Data

James, Marie, 1926–1996.
    Orphan girl : the memoir of a Chicago bag lady / [Marie James] ;
as told to Jane Hertenstein.
        p.   cm.
    ISBN 0-940895-39-0
    1. James, Marie, 1926–1996.   2. Homeless women—Illinois—
Chicago—Biography.   3. Homelessness—Illinois—Chicago.
I. Hertenstein, Jane, 1958–  .   II. Title.
HV4506.C5J36   1997
362.5'092—dc21
[B]                                                                        97-45653
                                                                               CIP

*To the men and women*
*of Wilson Avenue*

# *Preface*

Most memoirs are written by great people who did important things. Readers are challenged with the potentialities
of humanity. We like to read about uncommon people who
rise to heights of leadership and change their world.

But there are people who do uncommon things about
whom few autobiographies appear. These people look for
food in other people's garbage, sleep in the alleys of our
cities—people for whom the American dream is a daily
nightmare. We may wonder, How did they come to this?
Why don't they just get a job? Why is alcohol their con-
stant companion? Perhaps we don't know the answers to
these questions because we wonder but do not ask, and
may not be prepared for the answers if we did ask.

When Marie James was a teenager, she wanted to write
a book. Many people have this dream, but few get the
opportunity to see it through. This book is Marie James's
memoir, and is perhaps the only dream of hers that came
true. These are her words as told to Jane Hertenstein, a

member of the intentional Christian community Jesus People USA.

Marie affected many of our lives. To us, she was not just another one of the faceless, nameless bag ladies so visible on Chicago's streets. The Jesus People community tried to take her in, to make her life more comfortable, but she would have none of it. She was her own person. The reader will recognize idiosyncrasies, neuroses, and perhaps even psychoses in this book. These are *her* memories. We have checked the basic facts, but the impressions belong to Marie.

Through Marie's story we see an uncommon life, a life that touches others. She had courage and caring in the midst of degradation. Marie, an impossible tangle of humanity, had a personality that was endearing to those who stopped to talk with her. She cared about her friends. She could put on a concert if you gave her a piano. Some might say of her, "There but for the grace of God go I." But does that mean the grace of God is not within her also? And therein lies Marie's story.

—the editorial staff at Cornerstone Press Chicago

# *Acknowledgments*

Cornerstone Press Chicago wishes to thank several people who helped bring Marie's story to print. The many hours of taped interview were transcribed by Tom Montgomery and Renae Schneider. Rebecca Hill reviewed the transcriptions and filled in missing sections. Star Kolesar, Linda Meints, Jon Trott, Chris Ramsey, Katherine Williams, and Scott Knies added insights to the Marie who, for the last twenty-five years, walked the streets of Uptown, Chicago.

Dr. Michael McBride and Dr. Darrold Treffert were extremely helpful in giving details of the Wisconsin mental health system and what the hospitals were like when Marie was a patient there. Gerardo Dominguez, an adoption specialist with the Nebraska Department of Social Services, provided information on the child welfare system during the time Marie was in foster care.

We are exceedingly grateful to Alberta McBride who, with the help of assistants, combed the state of Nebraska confirming parts of Marie James's story. Her task was a difficult one as the James family moved around quite a bit. Through winter and spring snows in Nebraska she and her friends scoured cemeteries searching for family gravestones. She was able to piece together a genealogy of the family back to their origins in Wales. Bertie's efforts to substantiate a little girl's story—an old woman's memory— are an act of great kindness.

Thanks also to the staff at Cornerstone Press Chicago: Pat Peterson for cover design, layout, and copyediting; Tom Montgomery for comments that improved the book; and Teresa Wray for her encouragement and commitment to each of our projects.

Final thanks to the community and church of Jesus People USA, so many wonderful people who believed in Marie and in her story.

# Orphan Girl

*Nineteen ninety-five was the hottest summer on record in the city of Chicago; nearly eight hundred people died in July. The air was heavy, foul with the stench of rotting garbage coming in from the alley. You couldn't find relief anywhere.*

*Into the lobby of the inner-city mission where I live and work came Marie James—white haired, with blue sparkling eyes set in the midst of a wrinkled and dirt-tanned face. She had been coming to the mission for twenty years, looking for food and friendship. The mercury was already past 105 degrees, and I had no energy for giving. I wanted to be left alone and not have to face a promise I had made; I told Marie I would record her life story. I regretted that promise when I saw her pull into the lobby, her cart packed full of sour milk jugs and old newspapers. As we sat and chatted for a minute I saw cockroaches crawl in and out of old food stuff on her cart. It was all I could do not to abandon the project then and there.*

*Despite the extreme heat, the bugs, and the smell, I turned the tape recorder on . . . and it was magic. I began a journey in the cool Sand Hills of Nebraska. Marie's story transported me out of my present discomfort into another life, another time. It was a story that changed me.*

—Jane Hertenstein

# The Sand Hills

I was born in the Sand Hills of Nebraska, near a small town called Spalding. Robert Taylor, a famous movie star, was from around there. My father was John Robert James. His people were from Wales originally, but he was raised in New York City and grew up playing on the streets. I think that is where he learned all his wicked ways. The people from the Sand Hills were not like my father at all. They were a gentle people.

My mother's people were from Canada, but my mother, Alice Maude Mumford, was born in the United States. Her father was a successful farmer and had quite a bit of money for those days. He and Grandmother disapproved of my mother's relationship with John James, and refused to give her a penny when they married.

I grew up during the Depression. Many, many days went by when there was no food, just milk from the cows. In that part of the country a lot of people died of starvation. I never remember my father coming home with food, never any candy. At times he had money but he wouldn't spend it on us kids.

I know as sure as I'm sitting on this chair that God had His hand on me before I was even born. There were eleven children in our family. I was my mother's ninth child. One day my mother woke up, she smelled the coffee boiling and got sick to her stomach. She ran out onto the back porch and vomited green.

This is how my sister Faith told me the story. My father was gone, but that was nothing; he was gone most of the time. My oldest sister, Chloe, who was about nineteen then, was making cornmeal mush in a big pan, stirring it with a wooden spoon. Mother said, "Chloe, I'm pregnant. I'm not going to have this baby. You know what I'm going to do? The woman down the road had a miscarriage; she fell down. I'm going to go upstairs and jump out of the window." My sister dropped the spoon into the pan, "Mother, you're going to kill yourself."

"Well, so be it."

She went upstairs, sat on the windowsill, and let herself fall to the ground. She got the wind knocked out of her. She came in the house laughing, "I guess when I'm pregnant I'm pregnant clear up to my neck. I'm as pregnant now as when I jumped out the window. I don't know how we're going to feed this baby, but we're going to have to find a way."

I was born on a Saturday, May 6, 1926. Once my sister said to me, "Marie, you are going to shed a lot of tears in your life." I asked, "Why do you say that?" "Because it was misting outside when you were born. All the time Mom was giving birth it was misting." I laughed at her, "Oh, come on. I don't believe that crazy stuff." But it did happen. All my life I've been shedding tears.

⊠ ⊠ ⊠

My mother worked in the fields while Chloe did most of the cooking. Chloe was kind of retarded; she was that way since she was a few months old. The only time I remember seeing my mother home was when she was washing clothes on the washboard. She was always in the fields.

In the morning there was a mad rush to get out to the fields quick, but at night it was like heaven. When they'd call "dinnertime" everyone made a big dash to the table. People said it was for the food, but that was just half of it. My mother and brothers and sisters always had things to tell about what had happened during the day.

Father was seldom ever home. My mother was left two or three years alone running the farm and raising the children. Altogether in their marriage I don't believe my father lived with my mother for over six months. My mother and my oldest brother, Bill, ran the farm.

I'm not saying it was right, but several of the children my mother gave birth to didn't belong to my father. I know I am my father's child, but I know there are several who were not. Men used to come over. My mother was out on the farm, miles and miles from nowhere. I don't believe she was starved for sex; I think it was loneliness that pushed her. Yes, my mother was a very lonely person, even though she had all those children. I think she craved a man's companionship.

Also, she had so many children already, she might have risked sex, thinking she'd get food or other favors from these men. Maybe she thought one of the men would stick around.

I found all this out later from Faith. She told me how one time, when she was twelve and my brother was eleven, they peeked through the keyhole at my mother with one of her lovers. A man had come to the farm asking for a cup of coffee and they ended up in the bedroom. I was angry when Faith told me all this. I was quick to condemn my mother. Faith said, "Marie, you don't understand!"

She told me Mother was pregnant when she married my father. The baby was not my father's; they'd only been married about six months. He had not known her nine months. This was my oldest sister, Chloe.

One night, when Chloe was two months old, my mother and father were out in the barn milking the cows. My mother said, "The milk pails are getting full." There were only three milk pails. "One of us should carry the milk to the house and put it in the separator because we need more empty pails to finish the rest of the cows." My father said, "Okay, I'll take it in."

He didn't come back. He had walked into the bedroom, taken a pillow, and put it over Chloe's face. He was shouting at the top of his voice, "Die, you little bastard!" pushing harder and harder down on her face.

A man and a woman who had gone to school with my mother drove up just then in a horse and buggy. They saw a kerosene lamp burning in the house, so they walked in. In that part of the country people didn't lock their doors.

The man heard Father yelling and saw him trying to smother the baby. He said, "My God, John! What in the world are you doing?" My father turned around like he was in shock. He couldn't even talk. The woman ran past my father and snatched up the baby. Chloe was crying something terrible.

My father said, "I suppose you'll call the sheriff?"

They said, "No, we're not going to call the sheriff, John, but if we ever hear of you harming that child again we'll tell everybody."

So Father really had to watch his step after that. My mother never trusted him again. Whenever she went to the barn she always took Chloe. While she milked the cows she laid Chloe in the manger where the horses ate hay.

I apologized to Faith for being so quick to condemn my mother.

⊠ ⊠ ⊠

My grandfather must have forgiven Mother for marrying, as he was the one who usually kept us alive. During the summer it wasn't so bad, but there were long stretches in the winter when there just wasn't any food.

Once, when I was almost four years old, we hadn't had any food for three days. I remember jumping up and down and hanging onto my stomach, screaming. I didn't know what was the matter with me. My brother Jeff was looking out the window. He yelled out to my mother, "I can see a black speck moving down the section line and it's coming this way." My mother said, "Jeff, why do you say such things when it isn't true? Nobody is going to help us." She was sitting in a rocking chair with a white shawl around her. We were freezing cold. There hadn't been a fire in the stove for days.

He said, "Yes, I can see it!" She went over to look and exclaimed, "It's Grandpa!" Sure enough it was my grandpa coming with a lumber wagon. The snow was three feet deep.

He was still a ways away. "Go out and let him know we are alive." My brother—with nothing on his head, no coat, no shoes—waded in the snow clear up past his waist, almost up to his armpits; and he was big for his age; he must have been about eleven. He went through the snow and climbed up the windmill with a gunnysack. He got up there by the wheel where if the wind came up he could have been knocked off. He was hanging on to the windmill with one hand and waving that gunnysack as hard as he could with the other hand. Laughing. He must have been freezing to death.

He came into the house where we took turns rubbing him with snow until the color came back. I remember my grandpa pulled into the yard with the horses. There was shoes and coats, there was bedding, food, cough syrup. Everything on that wagon.

My big brothers and sisters carried stuff into the house. They put a big cardboard box on the table and one of them took out a loaf of bread. They just ripped it apart, stuffing bread in their mouths. Before they even swallowed one slice they were stuffing another slice into their mouths. I couldn't reach the box, but I was picking big pieces up off the floor and eating them as fast as I could. It tasted like fresh dough.

There wasn't any more to pick up off the floor so I stood on my tiptoes and tried to reach the bread. I got a hold of one great big piece when I felt the most terrible pain in my arm. It hurt something terrible. I looked down and my brother's face was on my arm. Bruce had bit me. He wouldn't open his mouth. "Why are you biting me?"

Finally, he let go to answer, "I'm biting you so that you will let go of the bread; it's the last slice."

I said, "No, no, I want it."

"Let go of it or I'll bite harder." So I let go. I went over by the window and cried and cried. The rest of the food Grandpa brought had to be cooked. I was sobbing my heart out. Bruce came over, "What is the matter, Marie? Why are you crying?"

"Because you don't love me anymore."

"Oh, but I do love you."

"No you don't, because if you did you wouldn't have hurt my arm the way you did."

"Marie, I didn't bite you because I didn't love you. I bit you so's you'd let go of the bread." He couldn't make me understand.

### Hiding in the Oat Field

My mother left my father because he was going to kill her and all us kids. The sheriff told my mother that she would have to sign papers to have father committed to the state prison. He said if she didn't sign the papers we wouldn't be able to get any food or rent money. So my mother went into town to sign the papers.

In town a man came up and warned her, "Alice, don't sign those papers because if you do you'll be dead, you and all your kids." My mother didn't understand what he meant so she went on back home. I remember the day. I remember the day my father came to kill us.

The same man came to the house and warned my mother that my father was coming. I didn't understand why we had to run. All of us, my mother and brothers and sisters, ran out to the oat fields. I got tired of running; I just couldn't run anymore; that's when my brothers tried dragging me. Faith said, "Oh, for gosh sakes, pick up that kid and carry her. If the wind is coming from the right direction her voice will carry down to the house where Pa is. He'll see us." My brother picked me up and carried me.

We were up high on a hill and we were able to look down and see my father. I peeked through the tall stalks to see what he was doing. He went inside the house and was calling for us, hollering out and cursing my mother. "Where are you, Alice? Where are you?" He called for each of us.

He looked for us in the house, then he went to the barn. When he came out with a shotgun and a box of shells I knew why we were so scared. He went next to the chicken coop, then he headed out towards the fields where we were.

I was hot and tired and began to whine. My older brother put his hand over my mouth but his hand began to sweat and I struggled harder. My little sister had grabbed some silver spoons from the house. When I saw her playing with them I wanted them. Mama told her to give them to me. Anything to keep me quiet.

My dad came so close to us I could hear him breathing hard and cursing. He called out each of our names again but none of us dared to answer.

Finally my father left. We could see him walking along the railroad tracks back into town. We were afraid to come out for fear he'd double back and find us. We spent almost all night in the field; it was dark when we snuck back to the house. My sister went to light a candle. Mother said, "No, no! Put it out. The neighbors will see the light, go to town, and tell Pa. He'll come back again." So she pitched it. Mother gathered up all us kids.

Dawn was breaking as we left.

It was June, the weather was beautiful. We were going to my grandfather's house, which was ninety-seven miles away. We hitched up the horses. One of the horses died along the way.

### All the Children Had to Go

Grandfather had a new wife whose name was Tillie. He had married her after our Grandma died. The arrangement this woman made with Grandpa was that she would marry him if she could have control over all the money in the bank, while my grandfather would have control of the property, the farm. My grandpa didn't like quarreling about money, so he gave in to her wishes.

Tillie didn't like Grandpa helping us when times were hard. She had told him, "If I catch you taking food over to your daughter again, I will take all the money out of the bank and leave you."

One day she had the Model T and was coming back from town. Grandpa had the lumber wagon and was heading to our place with food. She caught him. My grandpa was scared to death, but he went ahead and brought us the groceries.

Tillie was gone when he got back. She left with Doreen, their daughter, and all their belongings but she didn't bother nothing of his. She went into town and drew the money out of the bank and bought a hotel. The name of the town was Loretto. She was gone by the time we arrived to live with Grandpa. It would not have been possible otherwise.

We were free from my father but money was even shorter than before. To keep us alive Grandpa had to sell off all the hogs. Finally he lost his farm and had to lease a smaller place.

One day Tillie came out to Grandpa's new place. She asked my mother, "Don't you have a good-size daughter?" My mother answered, "Yes." Tillie said, "People tell me you're running low on food out here." My mother didn't want to admit it, but Grandpa came out of the bedroom in his long-legged underwear and said, "You know it's true." One of my brother's piped up, "Well, Faith eats the most."

"Ah ha, that's the one I want. The big girl, to help me run the hotel." My mother didn't want her to go. Grandfather and her got into a terrible argument. Grandpa said, "If you don't get rid of some of these kids we're all going to die here. Do you understand, Alice?" But my mother could not comprehend.

Faith was only thirteen.

My mother finally agreed to send her saying, "Faith, you'd better go. I'm afraid we're not going to make it." Faith was crying the whole time she was packing her clothes and all her little knickknacks. She was crying when she snapped the trunk shut and put it in the back of Tillie's Model T. She was crying when she turned around and shook her fist at my mother, "You might be getting rid of me now, but when I get big I'm going to get even with you. Then it will be your turn to cry."

Faith thought my mother didn't love her. My mother and Faith had had some misunderstandings before. She had been out more, to school and other places. She would come home and tell my mother, "Do you know other people don't live the way we do? We don't have curtains on our windows. We don't have a rug on the floor. We don't have any coats, any shoes. Do you know other people don't live like this?" My mother would just look down at the floor.

Faith learned to be a prostitute at the hotel.

### Meeting Davis

There was a man who came over to my grandfather's place. He was very handsome. I found out later that he was related somehow to Tillie. He wore expensive clothes and was talking to my mother, "Me and my wife, we don't have any children and we sure would like to have one of the kids." My mother said, "I don't think so, I feel afraid." My grandfather raised his voice, angry with my mother, "Alice, it doesn't make any difference how you feel or whether you like the sound of it or not." The man left.

About a month later he came back and again asked for one of us kids. My mother said, "No, I don't want to let any of my children go," but Grandpa said, "You have to, Alice, we're going to die here. I sold the last hog, we killed the last cow, and we've killed the last chicken. There's no more food." She said, "Well, we'll eat cornmeal." He said, "We're almost to the end of the cornmeal."

My mother looked up at the man with tears running down her face, "Which one do you want?" He said, "I want that little one over there with the dark hair and the big curls." It was me.

My mother motioned for me to come to her. I didn't know what was going to happen. "You are to go with this man." I was scared and started screaming, "No! No!" until the man finally left. She asked me, "Will you go with Grandpa?" In no time Grandpa had me in his Model T. I thought we were going for a ride. I thought I was going to come back, but I didn't. He dropped me off at this man's house.

There was a pretty lady at the house. She seemed nice but didn't show me a lot of attention. I thought they must have a lot of money because the house had fancy furniture and beautiful rugs and lamps. And they had running water and a sidewalk even though they lived out in the country.

It was warm and the screen door was open. I was playing by the door when I heard the sound of footsteps coming up the sidewalk. I jumped up and hid when I saw it was the same man who had been at Grandpa's. I ran through the dining room and into the bedroom. I peeked around the corner. He was looking right at me with a real nice smile. "Come here, I want to talk with you."

"Huh uh, no." He kept talking and coming a little bit closer. Finally, he squatted down, talking, "I'm not going to hurt you." It took a lot of coaxing, but finally I came over to him. He took my little hand and put it in his.

He said, "Please, don't be afraid. We're are going to be very, very good friends."

His name was Davis and I began to trust him.

As soon as Davis got off work he would come in the house, put his lunch bucket down, kiss his wife. He'd talk to her for a little bit, and then we'd go out the front picket gate for our walk.

I remember walking outdoors with Davis to many, many places in the woods. At the end of our walks we would go down the hill to a particular tree. Davis would play a game with me. He'd rest with his back up against the tree and his hands over his eyes. I'd run around and around him and the tree. Then I would peek through his fingers to see if he was looking. We always went to the same tree for our game.

One thing I'm absolutely sure of, Davis was not prepared for the innocence of a child. I loved Davis in my little girl way, and because he was so nice to me I'd do anything for him.

There had been sex play in my home between me and my brothers. I was so little I thought it was just another way to play together. Maybe I told him about this, maybe I gave him the idea. I'm not sure how it started. But whenever we opened that picket gate I knew we were going to the woods for our special games.

I was only four years old.

Late one night there was a big storm and the thunder popped. I screamed bloody murder and ran around the house looking for Davis. When I found him, I sobbed something terrible. He stroked my hair and said, "Marie, it was just a big noise. The thunder can't hurt you." He took me to the window; the lightning was going through the air. "That," he said, "is what can kill you."

The next evening we went down to our usual spot and the tree was lying on the ground. I was stunned. The white bark was showing. He told me it was struck by lightning. I said, "Davis, make it stand up." He laughed, "No, I can't make it stand up." I tried putting my arms around the tree but I couldn't budge it. I began to cry. "Will the birds come back again?" "No," he said. "Will the leaves rattle in the wind again?" "No. It won't ever rattle again. They're going to come and haul it away."

I remember one time out in the woods I was laying on a pile of leaves, sleeping. Davis had covered me with his black jacket. I woke up screaming.

He reached down quick and scooped me up. Patting me he asked, "Why are you crying? Did something scare you?"

I didn't know how to say the word "dream." I said the words "pictures in my head."

"What kind of pictures?"

"It was a tree, Davis."

"What kind of a tree?"

"I don't know—there was a thunder pop. The lightning came too, and a lot of rain. The tree went down. Then they came and hauled it away." I sobbed my heart out.

He said, "Oh, that was just a tree."

I said, "Oh no, no, Davis. It wasn't just a tree. The tree had a face."

"Huh? Whose face?"

19

I looked up and I said, "Yours."

I remember us playing in the water on the Fourth of July. I rode high on the back of Davis's neck while he waded through the water. We were out in a river, the Cedar River I think, quite some distance. This river was shallow but extremely dangerous. Very, very dangerous. Davis must've either been an excellent swimmer or knew the river very well because he did not seem afraid. He seemed very confident. And because he wasn't afraid I wasn't either. Water was whipping around us, whirling. It didn't just pass us, it swirled splashes, big splashes.

"Look," I pointed to something and said, "Davis, what's that?" It looked like a beautiful lady from the waist down in the water with a great big beautiful skirt. I said, "What is that? Oh, what is that?!"

He said, "It's a willow tree."

I said, "I am a tree." He said, "Oh, no you're not. You don't have any leaves." I looked at my arms. He said, "Come here, I'll show you." So we waded over to the tree. It took us a little while to get over there, that's how fast the water was moving. When we got to the bank, Davis reached up and pulled down a willow branch. "You see these leaves." I looked at the branch then I looked at my arms and said, "I don't have any leaves." And I began to cry.

He asked, "Why are you crying?"

I said, "Because I don't have any leaves; if I had leaves I'd be a tree." He reached up high and cut down a small branch and wove it into a crown. He then placed it on top of my head. I stretched both arms out and said, "Whee! I'm a tree!"

I thought being a tree was the most wonderful thing that could happen to anybody. I took some of the leaves off of the top of my head and put them on him and said, "Davis, you're a tree, too!"

When we got out of the water we reached for my underpants lying on a low branch.

I was standing in water up to my waist. We sat by the river and played a game. He had his knees up and his arms around his knees. I crawled under his knees pretending they were a bridge. He caught me between his knees and wouldn't let me out.

On the way home from the river Davis looked out into the distance. I had thought he was looking at something, but he wasn't really looking at anything. He muttered the words, "If ever I were to lose you." And then he stopped. "I'd rather be dead than to lose you."

As we walked up the hill, he seemed very sad. He was talking to himself. It was a steep hill and I tried to run ahead of him. I heard him say, "If only some good could come of this." He kept mumbling this over and over. Then he said, "Nothing ever will." To me they were just words; I was a kid.

Then I heard him laugh and snap his fingers. He was by a stump and called out my name. "Marie, Marie come here." I ran to him. He told me the strangest thing. It scared me to death. He said, "Marie, I'm going away." That's all he told me. I said, "I'm going with you."

"No, you can't go with me." I began to cry. He said, "Don't cry, please don't cry. Marie, where I'm going you can't come with me. One morning you will awaken; you will not find me. You are too young; you will never remember me."

One morning I guess I must have told his wife about our games. I don't remember though. I just remember she was standing by the sink doing dishes and I was pulling on her skirt and talking to her. Then she stopped what she was doing, dried her hands, and went to the wallphone. She cranked it and talked a while. She gave me a bath, put my clothes on, a little red sweater, and little patent leather shoes, and then she made me wait outside.

I heard a noise and I ran to the picket fence. I peeked through the fence and I saw a car come in the yard. I saw it pull in. Most of it was hidden but I could see a star on the door. I tried to stand on the fence to see over; it hurt my feet to wedge them in between the pickets. I hung onto the fence with both hands, "Hi, mister." He didn't answer me.

So I said it louder and again he didn't answer. I thought, "Well, I don't like you either."

I looked down the road and saw Davis getting out of a car belonging to a neighbor. He had his jacket over one arm and his lunch bucket in his other hand. When I saw him I began hollering, "Davis, Davis come find me." That was all a part of the game we played with each other. He looked up. Then he noticed the car with the star and he ran toward me. His face looked like a dead man. He put one hand on the gate and hit it open hard.

The policeman saw him coming and got out of the car. He met Davis just inside the gate. Davis got to me first and put me behind him. He was holding me with both his hands by my head. I had my fingers hooked through his belt loops.

The cop was a big fellow. He was very, very angry. He told Davis, "I have come for the child." Davis didn't answer. So he said, "I guess you didn't hear me. I have come for the child."

The kitchen door was open. Davis's beautiful wife had been peeking out the door all the time, watching. I felt something pulling me from behind. Davis's wife was trying to pry my fingers loose from Davis's pants. She took my hand and pulled me into the house. I fought against her, trying to get back to Davis.

In the house, we watched out the bedroom window. Davis's wife was standing behind me. Davis opened the gate but the policeman told him to go first. Davis said, "Oh, no, you're a police officer and you're in my home. I owe you respect. You go first." The policeman turned his back on Davis and walked back to his car.

I could only see half of the car from the bedroom window. The policeman was inside the car and Davis was standing there and they were talking. In those days there were running boards along the side of cars which you could step on to enter or leave the automobile. Davis had one foot up on the running board and one hand was on the car. He stood there talking to the policeman, it seemed like at least fifteen to twenty minutes, sort of a business talk in normal tones.

Then, all of a sudden, they began talking very, very loud. It was terrible. I didn't understand the big noise. I went to the kitchen door and tried to open it. I spent the rest of the day crying my eyes out and calling for Davis.

Davis's wife finally put me to bed. There was some sort of a cot in the kitchen. She laid me on the cot with all my clothes on, even my shoes, and covered me up. She left a light burning on a small table and went to bed.

When I woke up early in the morning, I was determined to find Davis again. I had trouble reaching the door knob, but I finally got it opened only to find that Davis was gone.

I was returned to my grandfather's house and it was from there I was taken to the orphanage.

*When I came into Jesus People USA as a nineteen year old I wrote about my life up to that point. I had really had a rough childhood. I had been raised in foster homes and juvenile centers and had received lots of abuse and mistreatment. Soon after Marie first started visiting our ministry, she read my story and began to ask everyone she met if Star was home yet. My husband and I were away at the time.*

*The afternoon we arrived home and parked our car in front of the Malden building, Marie was there waiting for us. She saw a lot of similarities between her story and mine, the things we'd gone through. She wanted to encourage me as a younger woman to make the good decisions that she had not made. Marie took me and my family under her wing. In some ways I think we replaced the family she had lost.*

*One day she gave me an envelope. She said I was to save it as a gift for my youngest son. Inside was a government bond in his name. She believed he would grow up to be a doctor and she wanted to help him be able to go to school.*

—Star Kolesar

When people get old they think about their childhood and my childhood really haunts me. I resent my childhood. I don't resent God, but still I wonder if it couldn't have been some other way.

We would have all been dead if my mom had not signed papers to send us to the orphanage. There was no food. None at all. I went to the Lincoln Home for the Friendless in October, 1931. I was five years old. I remember my first morning. I threw the covers back and jumped out of the bed. I told the girl in the next bed I was going to my mother. The girl said, "Your mother isn't here." I said, "Oh, yes, she is, my mother's here. She's on the other side of the door."

I had on a long nightgown and was barefoot. I went to the door, turned the doorknob, and went out. It wasn't my mother's kitchen at all; it was a strange place. There was a hallway and two long counters. I looked around and panicked.

I began screaming, "Mother, Mother, where are you?" A woman came out and tried to calm me, but I grew worse. I screamed and kicked and tore my hair out by the roots, but my mother didn't come. When I went back in the room, a woman told me to put my clothes on. I wasn't ever going to see my mother again. I wanted to run away. It was a moment I never got over.

On Valentine's Day, a teacher at the orphanage told us

we were going to make valentines. I didn't want to. So an attendant came over to help me. I still didn't want to. She asked me what I wanted. I said, "I want my mother." She helped me make a valentine, putting on glue, lace, and little paper flowers—very beautiful, except jagged where I had cut. After the valentine was finished, she said I was supposed to give it to someone I loved. I kept mine. I saved it to give to my mother.

I started walking down the road. The attendant ran after me. I said, "I'm going to find my mother." She said, "Your mama isn't down that road." She picked me up and took me back to the orphanage. I was crying real hard.

She set me up on a high counter. I was still crying. A younger girl there gave me a piece of candy and asked, "Isn't there somebody here you want to give your valentine to?" I said, "Yes, the janitor." He was a real old man, but he'd been nice to me.

"Well, why don't you give him the valentine?"

I went out in the yard searching for him. Eventually, I found him. He was raking leaves. I walked up to him. "Mister." I said it two or three times before he finally turned around. "Would you like to have a valentine? I wanted to give it to my mother, but they won't let me go find her. Would you like a valentine?" His face broke into a big smile. "I sure would." He looked really happy.

I left the orphanage in July, 1932; I was six years old. I wasn't as sensitive then as I had been one year earlier.

I was driven to my foster family—their name was Grayson—by a lady from the orphanage. She built my hopes up something terrific. She told me I was going to have a new mother and a new father. She said I was going to be very, very happy. I believed her.

When we arrived at my new home there was a little girl in the yard. I offered her a stick of gum. I had a whole package. I had chewed one, I had given a stick to the lady who was driving, and I offered the little girl one. The little girl didn't say thank you. In the orphanage they had taught us to be polite, so I waited a little while and then I said, "You didn't say thank you." She stuck out her tongue.

We went into the house and I ran up to my new foster mother and hugged her leg. She said, "Don't hang on me. Go outside because I want to talk with this lady."

I had a feeling she didn't like me.

I was outside only a few minutes when this little girl bit me three or four times on both of my arms. Then I saw the orphanage lady. She was already out of the gate and starting to drive away. I screamed at her, "Please don't leave me here. Please don't." I climbed up on the wire fence and I held my arms out to her.

## Call Me Mama

My foster mother's name was Eunice and her daughter's name was Cathy. Cathy was the same age as me; her birthday was in September and mine was in May. By the time we went to bed that first night, Cathy had bitten me another twelve or fifteen times. Teeth marks were all the way up my arms from my fingers to my shoulders.

When I got up the next morning I went into the kitchen. On the table was a cardboard box with toys in it. I had never had many toys in my life and I saw Cathy playing with them. I wanted one. "No, you can't have any of them." I asked why. "Because those are Cathy's toys."

Cathy pointed to the woman and said, "That's my mama, not your mama." I said, "I know that she's not my mama."

She said, "You don't have a mother, you don't have a mother or a father. You never did."

"I do, too."

"Well. If you have a mother, then where is she?"

I went to the window and pointed down the road and said, "My mama lives down that road."

Eunice overheard me talking about my real mother. She slapped me across the mouth. "Don't you ever, ever, mention your mother again. As long as you live in this house, you are to call me Mama."

I said, "No. No, you're not my mother."

She hit me across my back and shoulder. "I said call me Mama."

"You're not my mother." When I looked at my foster mother's hands I was petrified. I didn't know hands could cause such pain. My real mother's hands were always tender, gentle.

She started in on me with a stick and I didn't think she was ever going to stop. I kept jumping around and she kept hitting me—my legs, my ankles, my knees. My hips, my back, my belly, my chest, my arms. The very last one I got in the head and then I went down.

The next thing I remembered was that my right ear was itching. I put my finger in my ear and pulled it out; there was blood on it. Then I felt a pain in my side. She was poking me with her shoe. "Get up, get up, get up."

I turned on my side trying to get up. "I said get up."

Finally, I got to my feet. As soon as I got up I collapsed to the floor again. She gave me another whack with the stick. I had to hang onto the wall to get to my feet. Then she said, "Go out on the back porch and get a rag."

"What rag?"

"Get a scrub rag." She grabbed me by the nape of my neck and pushed me out to the back porch. She pointed to a rag hanging on a nail, "Pick it up." I did. "Now you go back into the kitchen and clean up that blood."

I was on my knees wiping up blood, but my nose was bleeding and my head was swimming. All I could see was the image of my mother's face.

Eunice told me to take the rag back out to the porch, but I guess I passed out.

When I came to, it was gradual. I heard my foster dad come in the back door. I heard the screen door slam. There was water on the back porch; he stopped for a drink and then stepped into the kitchen. As soon as he stepped over the threshold he said, "My God, my God, she's killed the orphan girl." I tried to speak but I couldn't. He picked me up.

Eunice said, "You aren't going to lay that bastard on my sofa."

He said, "Eunice, I've got to do something." So she put down some pieces of cardboard and an old blanket, and then let him lay me on the sofa.

My foster father's mother lived next door. He went over to get her. Grandma grabbed her bonnet and came real quick. When she saw me she said, "Get the blood off this child. I've got to check her."

My foster dad said, "Maybe we should call the sheriff."

"No, don't do that. They'll put Eunice in prison and us in jail, too, as accomplices. We'll lose our farm. Take off all her clothes." My foster mother wouldn't do it, so my foster dad had to.

Grandma checked me from the top of my head to the tips of my toes. She felt my head. "This kid has taken an awful beating. She's got a chipped tooth and a broken nose."

My arms and legs weren't broken, but there were terrible bruises. There was not a place on me that wasn't black and blue. Grandma was worried about internal injuries.

My foster dad asked, "What if she dies during the night?"

"Well, then we'll all go to prison. That's what will happen."

I didn't want to live. I recovered from that beating only to experience more. To this day I can't figure out why they didn't send me back to the orphanage. My foster parents, I know, didn't love me. I kept hoping. I never went to sleep at night without crying. I wanted my foster mother and my foster dad to love me more than anything else in this whole world.

### Say "Bastard"

I lived with my foster family for twelve years and it was like living in the pit of hell. The beatings were awful but the verbal abuse was the most painful. The third night I was in their home, she called me to come to her.

"Marie, come here." I had a little car in my hand. I didn't want to. She asked, "Do you want more of that stick?

I said, "No."

"Then come here." I walked up to her real slow with my head down because I was afraid of her. She said, "You're from an orphanage, do you know that? You're an orphan. Cathy's not an orphan, but you are."

"Do you know that all orphans are bastards?" I didn't know what that word meant. My foster father was sitting in the front room on the daybed reading the newspaper.

Eunice said, "You are a bastard. Now I want you to say it, say 'I am a bastard.' "

I wouldn't do it.

"Do you want more of that stick? Then say it."

I whispered, "I am a bastard."

"Now, I want you to say it louder, a lot louder." I did. "Say it as loud as you can."

I roared the words to where my stomach muscles hurt, "I am a bastard."

My foster father looked out over his paper and he said, "Eunice, don't you think you've gone just about far enough?"

### Grandma and Grandpa

I loved my foster grandmother; she was a real grandma to me. She taught me how to braid and she taught me how to sew. We spent a lot of time together and we shared many tender moments. I don't know how I could have made it without her. She was a jewel, a diamond.

My grandmother prayed. The first time I remember hearing my grandmother's prayers it was nighttime and she had on her nightgown. As she was praying she mentioned all her sons. There were four of them, their wives, and all their kids. When she came to my foster dad and Eunice, she mentioned my name. My name was mentioned in prayer, every night, all those years.

I remember Grandpa. He was a wonderful person, too. He'd hold me on his lap and sing to me. Jig me up and down on his knee. He was from Kentucky and sang a song that went like this:

*Out of the way for old Dan Tucker*
*He's too late to get his supper*
*Supper's over and his breakfast is cookin'*
*And old Dan Tucker just stands there lookin'*

Grandpa was senile and it was my job to follow him around. He was not allowed to go into the barn where he could get kicked by a horse; he was not allowed to go by the horse tank for fear he'd drown. Most everything else he was allowed to do, except wander off. So whenever he went toward the barn or horse tank, I'd have to run and tell Eunice. She would grab onto his hand and pull him away. The day Grandpa died, he was sitting in the front room in an old wicker rocking chair. It was Thanksgiving Day.

He said, "Nancy,"—that was Grandma—"Nancy, I'm going to the field."

"Yes, yes, my dear, my goodness."

He said, "No, I'm really going. Go get me my shoes and a clean pair of socks." She said, "Newton, you're not going anyplace. You're too blasted old."

Eunice was in the kitchen. She must have had a premonition, a soft heart, or something because she said, "I'm going to take him his shoes and socks."

He put them on. He wouldn't let anyone help him. He sat there—he really did think he was in the fields. He held his hands up like he was holding onto the reins. "Come on, Nell, let's go. Let's go, we've got to get this corn planted."

Then he put his hands in his lap. He was breathing very

heavy from all the excitement. He sat there quietly and then he tried to stand up, so Grandma got on one side and Eunice on the other. He yanked himself loose and got up by himself. He took off his straw hat and held it down in front of him. He bowed his head and said the Lord's Prayer. When he came to the end of it he said "Amen," sat down, put his head back, and was dead. A very sweet death. I knew Grandpa was gone.

He wasn't even buried a day when a man came over and said to get off the land. Grandma said, "What are you talking about? I own this land." He said, "Oh no, you don't. This farm was mortgaged and your husband didn't pay off the mortgage. You've got to get out."

Grandma was stunned. She asked my foster dad, "Can I go with you?" Well, he didn't know what he was going to do either. So she called her other son, Bruce, and went to live with him. That turned out to be quite nice. My foster mother used to go up there and wheedle Grandma out of her money.

### I Hid

At one time my foster father had played baseball for a living. He always told me he made a lot of money in his day. He stopped playing baseball after his father had a stroke.

My foster dad taught me so many, many lessons that I've used all my life. I think he should be given credit for this because my foster mother didn't teach me anything. My foster dad had a lot of faults, but I loved him so much and thought of him as my real father. To me he was like a god. I worshipped the ground he walked on. I later found out he was just a human being.

I worked outside with my foster father because Eunice and I fought constantly. He always took my part up until the time I reached puberty. After I reached puberty he went against me also.

I had to work like a dog, like a horse. Cathy, my foster sister, laid on top of her bed and read books. I worked from sunup to sundown. I milked cows in the morning and at night. I carried two buckets of milk, three gallons in each bucket, for a quarter of a mile. I hauled wood clear up to my chin in the morning and at night. I got muscles from lifting hay with a pitchfork.

I was a big girl. By the time I was eleven years old I was as tall as a grown woman and I came into my womanhood early. Eunice made the mistake of telling my foster dad. I wish she hadn't.

My foster dad tried sex with me. I was stunned. I guess I was about twelve. I was in the barn hanging up a milk bucket. I reached up to hang the bucket on a nail pounded into the rafters. I was wearing a pretty dress that my foster mother had made me; the only pretty dress she ever made for me. There were little decorations on the pockets.

My foster father came up behind me and put his hand inside my dress pocket. I was afraid, but I just stood there. I didn't know what to do. His hand slid over my belly and all I could think of was a rattlesnake. Shivers went up and down my spine, my whole body shook. It wasn't because I had any sex feelings, but because I was scared to death. His fingers touched my hair in the front and that did it.

I turned and I said, "Daddy, you don't have no right. You don't have no right to be touching me."

Boy, I ran out of that barn like the devil was after me. I hid behind the house. There was a small room attached to the house that was used in the wintertime to do some of the cold weather chores. I went behind this sort of shed thing. The milk separator was in there, and my foster mother came out to the separator and dipped some milk out of the separator bowl. I heard her ask, "Where's Marie?"

My foster father said, "Oh, I don't know, she's around here someplace." I could hear him talking. I heard him feeding the cats and talking to them. I heard the bucket scratch the barn wall as he lifted it to go feed the calves and pigs. I waited an hour until I heard him go in the house.

He asked, "Is Marie in the house yet?"

My foster mother answered, "No."

"I wonder where she is?"

"I don't know, she's really a peculiar girl. She's really a strange girl."

"Boy, you can say that again, she sure is an odd duck."

I knew Eunice wouldn't believe me. She'd kill me if she knew what had happened. It would be all my fault. I took off running through the woods, tripped on a branch, and fell down. I cut myself a good one, but I didn't stop; I kept right on going. I ran toward the field; I ran as fast as I could.

I stayed out in the field until late, maybe two or three o'clock in the morning. I didn't fall asleep. I thought for sure I'd fall asleep, but I didn't. In the early morning, when it was still dark, I heard my foster father coming for me with the dog. I saw his lantern swinging back and forth over the ground looking for me. His voice sounded far off, "Marie, Marie, where are you?"

The dog gave me away; he came up to me sniffing. Then my father came holding the lantern. He held the lantern up close to my face. He was crying, sobbing, "My God, my God, what have I done?"

I was crying, too. I loved him like my real dad. I just wish this hadn't happened.

"Come on back to the house, Marie."

I said, "No, Mama's gonna know. She'll know something is wrong."

He convinced me to come back. The sun was coming up. My heart felt very heavy. When I got home Eunice never said a word, never asked where I had been.

I went to bed for a few hours, but I didn't sleep. That was my first encounter. After that, there were more sexual advances.

### Lonely Old Farm

When I began my freshman year of high school, we moved to a small town in Nebraska called Bassett. It killed me to leave the farm. I hated living in town.

At first we lived in a little cabin outside of town. School was about four miles away. Cathy got to stay at a dormitory next to the high school, but I had to walk the four miles to and from school.

Daddy had stayed back at the farm. He and Eunice were having a fight. One day in late fall I told my foster mother, "I'm gonna go out to the farm and see Daddy." She said, "You're stupid enough. Go ahead and go."

I remember it was a Saturday. A very beautiful day and I was enjoying my walk. I loved the outdoors. The smells, the wind, the color of the sand hills. I always felt free when I was outside because that was when I was away from my foster mother.

There were a lot of things to see along the way. There were birds on the fenceposts, meadowlarks with bright yellow and black on them. They'd sit up on the fenceposts and sing, "See my pretty petticoat, see my pretty petticoat."

I loved the way the wind swept down, bending low the blades of grass, turning the windmill, water gushing up from the well into the troughs.

Living on the farm I always loved feeding the calves, milking the cows. In the barnyard, out in the meadows, the livestock knew me and loved me. Walking to the farm, I was excited about seeing my horse. He was old, but he was mine. His soft felty nose pressing into my hand looking for an apple or carrot.

I walked down the section, came into the yard, and the dog didn't come to greet me. I thought, "Gee, I wonder what's happened?" That dog was always with my father, never left his side.

Things were strangely silent. The windmill pump was shut off. There would be no water for the calves. I turned the pump on. Then I went into the barn to find my horse; my horse wasn't there. The barnyard was empty.

I walked towards the fields to find my horse. The fields were all grown up in weeds. I expected to see corn and oats growing, but there was nothing, nothing at all.

I went into the house. I found my father sitting alone at the kitchen table, looking miserable. In front of him on a plate were buckwheat pancakes, stiff as a board. I said, "My gosh, Daddy, is this what you're eating?"

He said, "Yah. I don't have anybody to cook for me."

I said, "Man, you're lucky you're not dead from this stuff." I felt sorry for him out here by his lonesome.

Finally I asked, "Daddy, where's my horse?"

He looked down at the floor and said, "I sold it."

I said, "Daddy, you didn't have no right to sell my horse. Where's the dog?"

He said, "I took him out and shot him." There was nothing left. All the cattle were gone. The chickens were gone, and everything else was just empty building.

I was sick to the core of my soul.

### I Can Sing

Eventually, we moved into a reasonably nice house right across the street from a doctor, Dr. Vinzer. But no matter how nice the house was, it was a place of horrible memories for me. I still feel sick just thinking about it.

When I began my freshman year I wanted my high school diploma so bad. English for me was as easy as falling off a log. I got two awards for penmanship. These were awards from the state, high awards. Yet it seemed to me my foster sister got the really good things. She went all over the state, writing for different things. That part really hurt me because I loved writing. I wanted to be a writer and someday write a book.

Also, it was in high school I developed a real interest in music. I learned to play the piano. I was in the school band and glee club. I found out I could sing. One day at school we had a Christmas program. My teachers encouraged me. They said, "Oh, let Marie up on the stage, let her sing."

My foster mother kept saying, "She can't sing, she can't sing." They argued with her. I got up on the stage; it was Christmas Eve. The teachers couldn't get me to stop singing. Every song I could think of I sang. They had to pull me off the stage. After I got home I paid for it. My foster mother slapped me around.

Another thing that never seemed fair to me; Cathy got to go to all of the football and baseball games. But I never got to go to any football games, or anything like that, because I had to work. I did babysitting and scrubbed floors for people.

It made me feel good to get away, but every time I crossed the threshold of our house my foster mother would say, "Okay, fork it over." I didn't get a penny of my money. She'd say, "You owe this to us. We took you in and gave you a home."

I also went down by the river to milk cows for people. I'd stop off by the sheriff's house on the way home and give them some of the milk. The sheriff, his wife, and their children became very good friends of mine.

### The Sugar Bowl

When I was fourteen I got a bad beating. I was washing the dishes, while Eunice was working in the garden, and Cathy was in the bedroom lying on her back reading a book. Eventually, Cathy came into the kitchen. The sugar bowl and butter and bread were still out on the table. She took a slice of bread and buttered it.

She had pulled a chair out partway and had her knee up on it, leaning over. While buttering the bread her knee slipped and so did the chair. The chair went over and her arm went down on the table. At the same time, she had her spoon in the sugar bowl and so the sugar bowl upset and rolled off onto the floor, breaking into a million pieces.

I began to pick it up, but then thought, "No, if I do that Eunice's gonna think I broke it." I said to myself, "No sir, I'm gonna leave that dirty mess on the table, and the sugar and the bowl just the way it is until Mama comes in. Then she'll know who broke the sugar bowl."

Eunice came in and that mess was the first thing she saw. She said, "Marie, did you break my sugar bowl?"

I said, "No ma'am, I didn't break your sugar bowl." She walked behind me. I had long hair. She grabbed ahold of my hair and pulled me over backwards so that I fell to the floor. She began kicking me at me and hitting me with all her might. I was on the table, then underneath the table. She finally quit kicking me when I was underneath the table.

I was sitting on the floor in the midst of the broken glass and sugar mess. Blood from the back of my neck and my nose and my mouth was dripping in the sugar. I remembered at school my teacher had written on the blackboard about sugar. She said sugar equals energy. I thought, well, if sugar equals energy, this doesn't make any sense. My blood's going into the sugar, that's my energy. My energy is going into sugar.

Eunice just let me sit there. I finally got enough strength to get up. I didn't even clean myself off. I walked right in the bedroom. I put my hands on the foot of the bed, and I looked at Cathy and said, "Cathy, how could you?"

### "This Hurt Me Worse"

One thing happened that stripped me of every bit of pride and self-respect. I came home from school. Eunice told me to go in and change my clothes and start to work. I went into my bedroom. I was so disgusted I just wanted to die. It came to the point that it didn't matter how much my foster parents beat me, none of it made any difference. I just hoped that someday they would beat me hard enough to kill me.

43

I went into the bedroom to change, but I couldn't find my dress. I just didn't care anymore. So I yelled out, "Where the hell is my dress?"

Eunice flew into the bedroom. "What did you say?"

I said it good and loud, "I said where in the hell is my dress?"

She slapped me across the mouth. "Don't you ever use that kind of language around here."

My foster father came in and Eunice told him what happened. She said, "I want you to give Marie a whipping."

My father came into the bedroom. He told me to lift up my dress and take down my pants. Now I was fifteen years old. When my foster father saw my privates I felt like he was drooling just like a dog over a piece of raw meat. God forgive me—I just wanted to kill him. Cathy was watching, laughing at me.

My father whipped me with his belt. Afterwards, he said, "This hurt me worse than it hurt you."

❈ ❈ ❈

I made it as far as my junior year. During my freshman and sophomore years, I got fairly good grades, but in my junior year I almost failed.

The verbal abuse at home was ten times worse than the beatings. Everything I did was wrong. I never did anything that was right. This sort of treatment convinced me that I was different. My foster mother had run me down so bad for so many years I believed I was different from everybody else on the face of the earth.

I had no self-confidence. If I saw someone coming down the street, I would cut across to the other side. I used to sweat under my arms until it spread down to my waist. And I stuttered so bad at school, it was pathetic. They used to keep me after school because I couldn't concentrate on my work.

One time I had to stay late after school. I was studying history about Mexico, 1854 or whatever. I was turned sideways in my seat with one leg under me and I started sobbing my heart out. My teacher came over to me. Her name was Jenny Near. She put her arm around me.

"Marie, whatever are you crying about?"

"Because I st-st-st-stutter and I sw-sw-sw-sweat underneath my arms so, so, so bad."

She said, "Marie, someday you won't sweat so much under your arms and people will take good notice of you."

I said, "I don't believe it."

"Marie, you have to believe it." This was the only thread of hope I had.

Another thing that bothered me were memories. Every time I passed a picket gate I panicked. I would forget where I was, who I was. My mind traveled to another place. Why did I feel so cold? These spells were like a seizure that came over me and numbed my mind and body. I tried suicide. I couldn't think of what caused all this pain. I knew something was wrong with me, but I didn't know what.

In high school, it would get so bad sometimes in study hall that I couldn't sit in my seat anymore. I'd go down to the bathroom. I'd pull my hair and bang my head on the wall. I can remember doing that. I was just a kid. Maybe sixteen or so. I remember pulling my hair out by the roots.

### I Fought Back

From the time I came to live with my foster parents they had forbidden me to talk about my real mother. So my family that I had known back when I was four didn't seem real anymore. That part of my life was only faint memories, things I couldn't really place.

So when Eunice told me that she had written to my real mother and had the address of one of my sisters, it threw me into turmoil.

She said, "We've supported you long enough. Soon you will have to be out on your own. Here's your sister's address." It was Faith's.

I wrote Faith a letter telling her how much I was suffering. Then I went out to mail it. Had I gone out the back door I think everything would have been all right, but I went out the front door. Eunice heard me and when I came back, she grabbed me by the hair and swung me around.

She said, "You've been out with some boy having sex."

I said, "No, I didn't. I just went out to mail a letter."

She said, "You're a liar. You've been out sleeping with some boy."

I couldn't believe what she was saying. I wasn't even

gone but maybe about ten minutes, because the mailbox was at the end of the block. I just had to go down to the corner and back.

Now I was interested in boys all the time, but I was scared to death of them. If a boy came around me I'd get so nervous I'd have go into the next room, but I wanted attention from boys. I wasn't thinking about sex; I just wanted somebody to notice me.

But it had been dark outside and Eunice was positive I was lying. She beat me something terrible. I undressed and acted like I was going to bed early.

She grabbed me again and said, "You aren't gonna sleep with my daughter; you've got syphilis."

I went into the other room and tried sleeping on the floor. She kept shouting and walking back and forth so I couldn't get to sleep, but I knew I had to go to school the next day.

What happened the next morning was the worst beating they ever gave me. The whole family jumped on me. I was just waking up when I felt my foster mother kicking me.

Then my foster father came out and kicked me with his shoe in the back. He said, "Get up."

Man, I hadn't done anything. I was just laying there sleeping. I said, "Please, don't kick me anymore. I can't stand any more beatings."

Then my foster mother came out and spit on me. We were in the kitchen. I think it was then that I started thinking they were going to try to kill me. I hit Eunice first. I took my fist and hit her in the middle of the back. She couldn't even straighten up.

Then I got my foster sister. The whole family was beating on me. I didn't want to hit anybody, but I was afraid they were going to kill me. I really was. I thought the whole bunch of them were going to kill me.

There was a tiny little hallway and my foster father got me into the bathroom. He started hitting me with his fists. I went down. I thought, "Uh-oh, boy, this is it for me," because he wouldn't stop.

He moved his foot near my head. So I sunk my teeth into his ankle. He yelled, "Let go," so I bit harder. The more he hit me, the more I sunk my teeth in. He stopped and I finally let go. I thought for sure he was going get me again before I could get out of that bathroom, but he didn't. Nobody hit me.

When I came out of the bathroom I had to walk past my foster mother. As I tried to get by her to go into the kitchen, she shoved me and my head went through the glass window in the back door. It cut a great big zigzag in my head and I was really bleeding.

It was time to go to school. So I went just like I was, covered with blood. I was limping and holding one of my arms that had been hurt. Both arms and both legs were black and blue. I had two black eyes. I had big knots on my jaws where they had hit me. I walked into the classroom and every kid turned in their seat to stare at me.

I hadn't even been in my seat more than five minutes

when the principal came over to me. I thought, "Uh-oh. Now what's up? I must have done something wrong." He sent me down to the nurse's station right away.

I was in there for a while getting cleaned up. I looked up at the clock. It was nine o'clock.

I said, "Oh, I gotta get up and get out of here. I have to go to my business class." I think it was junior business. "Otherwise, they are going to mark me absent."

She said, "No, please, don't worry about it. You're not going to be marked absent." Then she asked, "How often do you get these beatings?"

I said, "Sometimes everyday."

"How long has this been going on?"

I said, "Ever since I was a little kid."

The nurse was shocked. She told me to go on home.

### The Sheriff

I had just gotten home and walked into the kitchen when there was a knock on the front door.

Eunice took a key and she locked me in the back room, behind the kitchen. I could hear them talking. I stood up and tried to hear through the door, but I couldn't make out the words.

Suddenly I heard the sheriff say real loud, "Where's Marie?"

My foster mother said, "She's not here."

He said, "Oh yes, she's here, because I saw her go in the house."

He went to the door and it was locked. He said, "Mrs. Grayson, I'll give you five minutes to produce the key and unlock that door."

She said, "I don't have the key."

"If you don't produce that key within ten seconds, I'm going to take you to jail."

"Oh no, you can't take me to jail," she said. "I'm a Christian. I belong to the church."

The sheriff repeated, "I'm going to take you to jail."

Right away, Eunice took the key out of her apron pocket and pulled the door wide open.

When the sheriff saw me, he grabbed a chair. He said, "I cannot believe what I am looking at."

My foster parents were both high-standing people in the community. Very well respected. The sheriff said, "I'm going to leave, but if I ever find out that this child has been beaten like this again, I will arrest both you and your husband."

After that, I never got any more beatings.

※ ※ ※

My foster mother took me to Omaha, Nebraska. She dumped me me just like a piece of garbage with my second oldest sister, Faith.

When Faith saw me, she stood still for a minute. She looked at me and leaned her head one way and then the other. Then her mouth flew open and she began running with both her arms out. She said, "My little sister, my little sister!" Faith hugged me so tight.

My arms hung down at my sides. It had been twelve years since I last saw any of my family. I was in shock.

"Oh Marie, oh Marie," she said.

I asked, "Are you Faith?"

She said, " Yes, I'm Faith, your big sister."

I moved in with Faith and I tried hard to understand her life, and the pressure she was under. She worked hard and had two small children to raise—a little girl, four, and a little boy, one. There was nothing in this world I wouldn't have done for her.

In Omaha, I gradually stopped stuttering. When I was away from my foster mother and the verbal abuse, I talked just like other people. For the first time in my life I started to feel like a human being. It was a millstone off my neck.

While I was living with Faith, Eunice came to get me. She said, "Marie, I'm taking you back to Bassett."

By that time I had smartened up considerably. I told her, "Well, I'm not going back."

She said, "Marie, you're underage. I can force you to go."

"If you force me to go back, I'll either kill you or I'll run away."

She didn't say one word. She just walked out the door.

I really thought everything was going to be okay living with Faith, but she had a live-in boyfriend and she started thinking this boyfriend and I were making out. Maybe she thought that her boyfriend would eventually force me or something, I don't know, but anyhow she told me I had to leave. I was seventeen years old.

I did go back to Bassett because I wanted to finish my senior year.

Once I was back my foster mother never let up. She kept telling me I had syphilis. I don't know why she said this but I finally moved out of the house and lived with a neighborhood family.

The lady who took me in was real sweet to me. I milked her cow, scrubbed her floor, helped take care of her little boy, and other odd jobs to pay for my room and board.

One day while I was doing housework at another family's house, my foster mother came by. She wanted to take me home. I was barefoot and needed to wash my feet before I could go. She came in the kitchen and shook her fist at me saying, "Hurry up, hurry up." She got me so nervous I almost upset the pan of water I was scrubbing the floor with.

Ira, the man of the house, was in a wheelchair, and he said, "For God's sake, Eunice, let that kid alone. Let her wash her feet so she can go."

I began crying, "Ira, I don't want to go. She beats me. Please don't make me go with her."

My foster mother cut loose on Ira.

He said, "You don't talk that way to me in my house, Eunice. You're gonna leave without this girl whether you like it or not."

She said, "Well, she happens to be my daughter."

Ira said, "I don't care. You don't know how to treat a poor

little girl. That little girl would do anything for you if you gave her love, but you give her hate."

She replied, "I can't love her; she's a bastard."

Later, Ira's wife told me about my foster dad. We were in the kitchen having a cup of coffee and talking. She told me I should know the truth. My foster dad was going to bed with almost every woman in town.

When she told me that, it was the end. I felt sick to my stomach. I think I still loved my foster dad even though he beat me and tried to have sex with me.

"I don't want to hear these things you are telling me."

She said, "Marie, come on back and get your money."

I didn't want the money. I didn't want anything to do with either my foster mother or my foster father anymore. No wonder Eunice suspected me of syphilis. I think the only reason she came to Omaha to get me was to stop the gossip.

⊠ ⊠ ⊠

Later I learned that my foster parents left Bassett. I believe they were run out of town. People in the Sand Hills are like that. My foster mother, I really don't believe she had any friends. I think people just tolerated her. She used to say the most terrible things about people. She used to start gossip. I know she made a lot of enemies. People like to talk, that's only human, but she could cause more trouble in one block in five minutes than any woman I ever saw.

Eunice's religion was a very sick, sick, sick religion. I knew I never wanted to be a Christian because my foster mother told me she was a Christian.

After I got saved, every time I prayed I could see my foster mother's face and I knew I had to forgive her. I still resented her. I knew I had to forgive her, but I couldn't find a way. I often asked God why I had to endure my foster mother and the beatings. Why did I have to suffer?

### *The Boy I Wish I Had Married*

I was glad to be away from my foster mother and father. Slowly, I started to gain self-confidence, I stopped stuttering, and no longer had a big perspiration problem under my arms.

I hadn't graduated from high school. I went back to Omaha in 1943, and lived with Faith for a while. Eventually, I got a room downtown. The big city scared me. I hated living alone, but I was learning my way around. While living on my own, I had the mumps. A young woman who lived at the end of the hall helped me a great deal.

I found a job at Armour Meats. One funny thing happened right after I got my first paycheck. This check was for twenty-four dollars. I went into Woolworth's dime store and spent every bit of it except for one nickel and one penny. I was loaded down with parcels making it difficult walking to the bus stop. It was there I discovered I didn't have the fifteen cents bus fare. There was an old man waiting at the stop. I said, "Sir, I'm ashamed to tell you this," and I began to explain to him how I had spent all my money except for one nickel and one penny. He asked how old I was and I told him seventeen. He gave me fifteen cents to get home on.

At work I met a boy I wish I had married instead of my husband. His father was a hotshot at the plant. He was a smart boy and a lot of fun. He had finished high school and was getting ready to go to college when the bombs were dropped on Pearl Harbor. I don't know if he liked me, but I liked him a lot. I just didn't know how to show it. I never learned how to act around boys.

This boy came to my apartment one day. He had been drinking. He asked if he could lie down on my bed and I said, "I don't care, go ahead." I was sitting on the side of the bed. We were talking and smoking cigarettes. We also shared a quart of beer. He fell asleep on my bed.

He woke up; we talked for a while and then he left. I never saw him again. One of the kids at the plant told me he had gone off to war. I cried for about two or three weeks. I missed him.

*I had many opportunities to take Marie home and carry her cart up two flights of stairs and she'd go, "No, no, you just stay down here and you go." And it's like two tons. But I'd carry it up. There was one night in particular where we had some freezing rain that left a lot of ice along the streets and sidewalks. It was very hard to walk. We were getting out of the van and there was an old man who was coming up the other way and he kept slipping. So I said, "Marie, I am going to help out that old man." And she said, "Oh, you go out there and get him, you get him upstairs right away." So I helped the man up the stairs to her home. Her door would only open up so far. I remember getting her inside and then him. He sat down and . . . well, Marie loved to smoke. Two things that she loved the most were Jesus Christ and her smoking. But all I remember is just getting her cart in and her lighting up her cigarettes and getting in this man's face and saying, "You know what, you need to receive Jesus now! Right now! He's been so good to me. Look at me. I'm a wretch, I don't deserve anything, but Jesus helped me; you need to receive Jesus, too."*

*It is just amazing that as soon as she introduced herself, she just went right to the core with everybody. With anybody. She did with me, too.*

—Scott Knies

## A Terrible, Terrible Life

It was loneliness that drove me to my husband. I didn't really love Ray Grine, but I was so lonely—I just let my emotions take over. At first it was very exciting to have someone. Ray was older, about thirty. He was someone to laugh with and talk to; he understood my inexperience.

My husband looked like a Portuguese sailor. He wasn't handsome, but nice-looking. He was one-quarter Irish, one-quarter American Indian, and one-half Negro. His sisters were dark, but Ray was light-skinned with blue eyes. His hair was kind of fuzzy and he had a big nose, but except for that you wouldn't believe he was part Negro. But my friends knew. I lost every one of them when I married Ray.

The state of Nebraska was home to a lot of prejudiced people. Maybe not so much now, but back then they were. Children were raised to hate, to disregard anybody that wasn't their own kind. I know that was how I was raised:

hatred for the black person, for the Indian. I didn't understand how deep this hatred was until it was too late.

If I had been wise I would have left Ray the very day we
got married, but I wasn't smart. Things I didn't realize at
first became clearer the longer I was married. Gradually,
little by little, Ray began to frighten me. My life with him
was a terrible, terrible life.

I didn't love him, but I thought I was pregnant. Going
to the doctor to be checked never occurred to me. Fearful
of pregnancy, I had to threaten Ray in order to get him to
marry me. I was seventeen and underage. It was against
the law in Nebraska for a man to have sex with a minor.
Ray knew he had to marry me. After we were married I
realized I wasn't pregnant after all.

Some good did come from our marriage. Because I had
worked outside all the time with my foster dad, I didn't
know how to keep house. Ray taught me how to cook and
how to make a bed. Ray taught me self-defense. I hated
every bit of it. Once he handed me a knife and said, "Okay,
try to stab me." I said, "Ray, I don't want to learn all this
crap." He would answer, "Do it, now. What would you
do?" I'd grab the knife and hold it up in the air. "Oh,
Marie, you don't ever want to do that. Somebody could
grab your wrist and get the knife away from you and kill
you. Hide the knife in your belt and bring your arm up real
slow; when you bring your arm up, bring the knife with it,
and you get them in the belly." Later on, I was able to put
to use the things he taught me.

Ray and I had children, beautiful children. They did not look black at all. All my neighbors said I was going to have a black baby, like that was a bad thing. I knew I would love the baby whatever color it was. Ellen Rae Grine was born in 1944. She was a very beautiful girl. All the rest of the babies in the hospital were beet red, but she wasn't. She was the whitest baby I ever saw.

When the nurses brought her to me from the nursery I carefully unwrapped her. I don't know why, but I'd always unwrap my baby and look her over. From the top of her head to her toes. One day, they brought me a baby that wasn't mine. This baby had my baby's face, but when I unwrapped her she had skinny legs. Ellen had fat legs. There was no nurse around; they were all so busy running back and forth. I called two or three times, but no one would stop. Finally, I wrapped the baby back up and laid her at the foot of my bed. I passed the time reading a magazine. A nurse came over to me. "Mrs. Grine," she said, "you are not feeding your baby."

I said, "No, I'm not going to feed that baby. If you will give me time, I'll explain why," but she walked off and left me. Two interns came in and said, "Mrs. Grine, have you ever thought you needed to see a psychiatrist?

I said, "Not recently, no."

They asked, "Do you know what we do to mothers who don't nurse their own babies?"

I answered, "No."

"Well, we put them in a mental ward."

I said, "I don't think I deserve to go to a mental ward."

"We're gonna call the head doctor in here and as soon as we get the head doctor, we're going to take you straight to a mental ward."

That scared the daylights out of me. They wouldn't give me a chance to talk. I tried to tell them that was not my baby, but they wouldn't let me talk. The head doctor came in and looked at me. "Mrs. Grine, why won't you feed your baby?"

I told him, "Because this is not my baby. My baby has fat legs and this baby has skinny legs." He turned the baby over on its back and read the name, "Gonzales."

He said, "Oh, my God, this baby belongs to the Mexican woman on the other side of the hospital." Ellen came back. Her mouth was filled with milk. Milk was running down the side of her mouth. But Ellen wouldn't suck off of me. I couldn't even cry, I was so mad. Ever since I was eight years old, I dreamed of holding my baby and feeding it.

### Baby Douglas

I had two daughters with Ray. The first one I named Ellen Rae (Rae after my husband), the second daughter was Lilith Marie (Marie after me). Lilith was born in 1945.

Then in 1947 I had a little boy, Douglas Wayne. He was something else. I used to hold him on my knee and jig him up and down. He'd throw back his little head and laugh. Oh, how he would laugh. Ray would be reading the newspaper and yell out at me, "Be careful, you're going to snap that baby's head off." Douglas was so much fun to play with.

I went to work shortly after I gave birth to Douglas. I didn't want to work, but I had to. Ray worked nights and I worked days. Every morning I went to work I'd cry. I'd kill myself trying to get home to see my children. I couldn't get home fast enough.

One day—it was a Saturday—I had a peculiar feeling when I left the house. I had the day off and needed to run some errands. I left the baby in his little basket in the yard with Ray. I took the two girls with me to the shoe repair store over on Corby Street. I had some work shoes that needed new heels. I was gone for two or three hours.

I was coming home with my two little girls running on ahead of me. A little colored girl—she had the sweetest little face—she ran up to me. She said, "Miss Marie, Miss Marie, something's happened to your baby. Something real bad, it's bad."

I looked at her face and knew she was telling the truth and started running. When I got to the yard I saw the basket, but it was empty. I ran up on the porch and about nine Negro women grabbed me by the arms. My baby was on Pearl's lap—that was my husband's sister—she had the baby turned over and was hitting him on his back with the flat of her hand. While we were standing there the rescue squad came in. I tried to get to my baby, but they wouldn't let me. I said, "Please let me hold my baby."

I got on my knees and prayed. I said, "God, if it is your

will, please save my baby's life." They had the suction cup under his nose and mouth. I could see his little tongue coming up into the suction cup; it was blue. I knew he was gone.

They wrapped him up and covered his face. Ray and I got into the ambulance with the baby. I begged them to let me hold the baby—I wanted to hold him even after he was dead—but they wouldn't let me.

We got to the hospital. They had put my baby on a little cart and I walked right behind it. I was much more calm than my husband. He looked like a dead man; he looked more dead than the baby.

The head doctor came in. He took hold of baby Douglas's wrist. He looked up at the two interns and shook his head "no." I went out and told my husband. I said, "Ray, little Douglas is dead."

My husband went crazy. He jumped up and smashed his fist through the wall. Knocked a great big piece of plaster off of it. He was talking and acting crazy. People just stood looking at him. Finally, he quieted down a bit.

While in the waiting room, two detectives came in. They said, "You killed that baby didn't you? Admit it, you killed him." They just kept saying that to me. I told them I wasn't even home at the time, I had left the baby with my husband. The policeman came and took us home. The doctors warned them, "Don't be alarmed by what the husband does, it's the woman you should watch. She is too quiet. She might go berserk or do something crazy."

But I knew they were wrong.

After the baby's funeral I went to the coroner. I cried the whole way there, cried the whole time I waited for him, and cried while I was talking with him. Before the funeral I had signed papers for an autopsy. I asked him, "What caused my baby to die?"

It was his heart. A congenital heart condition, meaning his heart was damaged at birth. I didn't believe it. He might have a little bit of congenital heart damage, but it wasn't like what they thought it was at all.

I was twenty-one years old when Douglas died in 1947. I wanted to save my marriage, not because I was taught that a man and woman should live together no matter what, but for the sake of my children. My children loved their daddy. When they cried for their father it would just tear me apart. But I could not live with Ray. Maybe it was fear or the hurt of losing my little boy. I was so depressed, I just had to leave.

### Tomorrow

I was pregnant again, but couldn't catch hold of life. My mind was in a fog. I left my husband and wanted nothing more than to live quietly my own way. Funny how things happen.

I longed to see my mother again—it was an odd kind of hope. I had heard she was living in San Diego, California. So I went to see her with my two little girls.

I arrived in a taxi. I had two suitcases, a huge purse,

shopping bags, and the two girls. I had the address, but before I even got to the door I saw a woman coming down the street. She looked like me. She walked up to me and gasped, "Oh, you're one of my children."

I said, "Yes, I am Marie."

She grabbed me so hard I couldn't breathe. My arms were hanging like sticks down at my sides. She was a stranger, and I didn't know how to hug a stranger. I just left my arms hanging limp. Then she released me a little bit and I said, "This is tomorrow."

In the orphanage I used to cry every night for my mother. A pretty young attendant used to comfort me by saying, "You'll see your mother again."

I would sob, "No, I won't. I won't ever see my mother again."

"Sure you will, honey. Tomorrow. You will see your mother tomorrow."

"When is tomorrow?"

"Tomorrow," she said, "is the day you will see your mother."

### That One White Day

I tried to ask my mother questions. Questions about the past, about my other brothers and sisters, about why she gave me up. As soon as I began to ask questions, she'd go off in another world. I thought, "I'm never gonna find the answers to the things I want to find out." I could not take up where we left off when I was five years old.

I was awfully depressed. I remember rolling on the bed one day pulling my hair out; I couldn't even cry. If I could have cried it wouldn't have been so bad, but I couldn't even shed one tear. My mother came in and asked, "What's the matter?" I tried to explain to her, but I couldn't make her understand.

She said, "I can't stand to see you suffer like this. Marie, I want you to forget that I'm your mother. You know how to pretend, don't you?"

I said, "Yes."

"I want you to pretend that I'm a very good friend. I live just down the street and you've come to visit me." She asked me to get up and get dressed. I didn't feel like getting dressed. She made me get dressed; fresh makeup, hair combed. She said, "I'm taking you out for the day, across the San Diego Bay."

We walked up to Main Street; the cars were coming in both directions. We cut across the street and walked down to the wharf. My mother bought two tickets for the ferry. There were cars on the bottom of the ferry. I was thinking about my dead baby, about my marriage on the rocks, my foster parents.

There was a small snack shop on the ferry. On the upper deck in a small dining area we sat down at a table. The girls were dressed real cute, their wavy black hair tied back with ribbons, and white eyelet dresses with little white slips underneath. We made quite a family portrait up there on that ship.

My mother ordered three great big slices of cherry pie each with a scoop of ice cream on top. What a delicious sight, that red cherry pie with vanilla ice cream perched delicately on the crust. I put my fork up to my mouth a couple of times and immediately put it right back down. That happened four or five times. My mother was curious about what I was doing.

"Every time I put my fork to my mouth, the baby in my belly kicks me real hard."

She laughed, "The baby just wants another bite." I thought I was going to split. I laughed so hard. My mother was laughing too, roaring. We had a ball going across the bay and back. On the way back, my mother bought a fish. We carried it home in a soggy newspaper and ate it that night for supper.

I'll remember that day always. It will forever be a white day where there was a lot of air and a lot of light. High waves as the ferry plunged us across the bay, and laughing on the open deck into the wind.

### Laughing Always Makes You Feel Better

My mother found out I liked tea. She would serve me tea in her backyard where there was a wonderful garden. It was like walking into the garden of Eden. She had a waterfall she made with her own two hands. She knew I loved that backyard. She would say, "Take your cup of tea out there and sit on the love seat. Sit there alone."

She would come out later to sit and talk with me. She

would say, "No matter how you feel, laughing always makes you feel better." I liked hearing that.

My mother had a way of making people feel better about themselves. She showed them how to laugh at life, at little things. I remember the love she showed her friends and neighbors.

One person she helped was a young man she had befriended. He had double pneumonia and was sent home from the hospital to die. He lived right around the corner from my mother. I was coming home from work one morning and saw my mother coming down the sidewalk with a big smile on her face. The sun was just coming up, a huge sunrise behind her head, and she was grinning with one tooth missing on the side. In her hands she carried an old cracked plate and a great big bowl. There was steam coming out of the bowl.

I asked, "Mother, what have you got?"

She said, "Chicken broth."

"Where in the world are you going with that chicken broth?"

"I'm going up to Ed's place. He's got double pneumonia. I want to do something to make him feel better."

After I got home I fed my kids and while they were busy playing in the backyard, my curiosity got the best of me. I thought, "I'll leave them just for a second." I ran out of the yard and around the corner. There was a huge flight of stairs. I tiptoed up the stairs because I didn't want my mother to know I was spying on her, but I was. I peeked around the corner into a bedroom.

There was a man, young, but old. His face was all sunk in and his hands looked like they belonged to a person of eighty-four years old. He was propped up with seven or eight pillows. He was eating my mother's chicken broth. My mother was sitting by his bed with her back to me. I could tell she was laughing. He was laughing so hard he could hardly eat his soup. I started to say something, but didn't want to ruin the scene. I stood there for ten minutes, watching them laugh and talk.

This man got well. I don't know if it was the chicken broth or my mother's laughter. It might have been the two of them together, but soon he weighed two hundred and sixty-five pounds. I heard later that he bought a ranch, married, and raised nine kids.

My mother had a magnetic personality. If you saw her once and talked to her you would always be anxious to see her again. She was quite a gal. If I showed you a picture of her you would say, "What an ugly woman." I saw my mother's wedding picture and she wasn't pretty. She had naturally curly hair and big brown eyes. Her face was kind of skinny. I talked to my older sister about our mother and she said, "You're right, Marie, she wasn't pretty when she married. She started to blossom when she was thirty years old. All those ugly bones that stuck out in her face eventually made her very beautiful."

In California I found I enjoyed falling asleep to the foghorns, blowing all night long across the bay like a lullaby. One time my mother took me and the children to an arboretum. There were flowers there from all over the world. One strange plant was a Venus flytrap. A fly would land on the leaf of this plant and the leaves would quickly attack the fly.

There are many precious moments that I remember with my mother in California. At the time it didn't seem like very much. Now that I am older, it hurts. When I lay down and dream, there are times when my heart beats for wild joy because I lie there and remember all the marvelous things I saw and did.

Another happy time we went down to the ocean to pick seashells. Mother found out I liked seashells. For those few hours I forgot all my troubles. There were tears of pure joy because growing up I never thought I'd get to see the ocean. I remember one time with my foster father we were standing by the fence line feeding the calves and I asked him, "Daddy, do you think I'll ever get to see the ocean?" He said, "Maybe someday when you get big you will." But I never thought I really would.

At the seashore I unhooked my nylons from my garter belt, took off my shoes. I waded into the ocean watching for the tide because I had heard about ocean tides. The water was ice cold, but I didn't care. I wish I could paint this picture: There was a huge boat that sat way out in the harbor. The sun was going down behind my mother's head and she looked beautiful. Delicately she picked up her dress to keep the hem from getting wet.

I said, "Mom, put your dress down, I can see your petticoat."

She looked like I had slapped her. She said, "I just
washed this petticoat this morning and it's as white as
snow." She was like a little girl. My mother looked out
across the ocean, then she looked at me. She said, "Oh,
Marie, I wish life could go on forever just like this. You and
me, and the two babies."

### Point Loma

After some time I moved out of my mother's house and
was living alone. I thought I could pick up where I left off
with her, but too much water had gone over the dam. My
mother's new husband and I had gotten into a terrible
argument. I couldn't come there in the evenings, just in the
daytime. He had thrown a knife and barely missed my little
girl's head. I think he was an old Irish sailor. I rented a very
small apartment right around the corner. There was a girl
I met there; she was the sweetest thing. She watched the
two girls while I worked as a waitress at Point Loma.

Oh, what a dining room that restaurant had! Huge windows from the ceiling to the floor that looked out over the
ocean. People sat in the lounge, sipping drinks, and
watching the yacht races. Colorful sails dotted the bay. It
was a magnificent dining room with a stone fireplace at
one end where guests sat with blankets wrapped around
them because their boats had overturned in the races. I
worked hard carrying great big heavy trays over my head.

One day I returned home from work. I got off the street-car and went up to my apartment. My kids were gone. Somehow my husband, Ray, had found us and had taken my children. My friend was in hysterics when I came home. She said, "I tried to save your children, but I couldn't. Your husband threatened me with a gun." My oldest daughter was about three at that time, my other little daughter was one year old. My husband was not an alcoholic, but he was overly possessive and extremely jealous.

Right after this, I went back to retrieve something from Point Loma. I don't remember if it was my purse or pay-check or what. I was in a daze, very lonely, and very scared. I felt completely hopeless and helpless. Then I met this man. I don't remember where I met him, maybe the bus stop. We went to a bar. After that we went to a hotel and got a room. At the hotel, we ordered room service, some coffee, and sandwiches. I took off my expensive two-piece suit, and placed my hat, gloves, and earrings on the hotel dresser top. I had nothing on but my petticoat, bra, britches, and nylons. He was bare to the waist, but still had on his pants and socks.

We sat and talked for a long time. I thought about suicide. I wanted my kids and knew my marriage was gone forever. I had quit my job. I guess that is why I went back to Point Loma. It was hard, exhausting work. I didn't fit in with the waitresses, there was a lot of swearing. I didn't like my boss at all. He had told me not to bother to come back to work if I wouldn't let him come up to the hotel room also. I just quit on the spot. Then I was afraid I wouldn't be able to find another job. The man and I talked about what would happen if I returned to Nebraska. I just couldn't go back, the memories were too much for me.

After this man left, I took a real good shower. I shampooed my hair and sat on the bed brushing it out. I told myself, "Whatever happens to my kids, I guess it will happen. They are away from me. I can't stop it." Everything left my mind—my children, my marriage, my job. All I wanted to do was rest.

I slept in the nude and watched the ocean from the hotel window. I slept for fourteen hours straight. I stayed for two days, mostly sleeping. I was exhausted physically and mentally. Those days in that hotel room all alone were so peaceful. I looked out at the ocean; I couldn't see much of it, but I knew then, there's got to be a Creator. There's got to be something that keeps the world and this water the way it is.

### The Red Ocean Water

When I left the hotel I was all dressed up. I went to the bus stop and got on the wrong bus. I had to take another bus back and out again. The street was called Ocean Beach. I looked out of the bus window and I could see the ocean. I decided to get out and walk back to the ocean's edge. I stood by the shore, weeping like a child.

The sun was a fire red. It was burning like a ball of fire. It was going down and the ocean was a red light all the way

74

across, all the way up to me. At first I felt frightened because it looked like the whole world was water. It was the most beautiful sight I saw in my entire life. I stayed in that water quite awhile and I was having a ball all alone. Not once did I feel alone. I was very happy.

⊗ ⊗ ⊗

I thought I better get out of this dreamworld I was in and get back to reality. I went back to my apartment, took off my good clothes, and put on a dirty cotton dress. I thought: "I gotta get another job, gotta get this apartment cleaned up," but I laid on the bed. The only time I prayed was when the sorrow was more than I could bear. Thinking about a new baby did give me a little hope. Maybe this one would live.

There was something very strange about this child I was carrying. I never had morning sickness. With all my other children I had terrible morning sickness, but this baby seemed to have a special blessing on it even from the first.

After awhile my neighbor, the young woman, came over. She invited me over for coffee and I sat there and talked. She asked me if I was moody. I answered yes. She took me for a walk. It didn't help much, but a bit. Then I came back.

I was there two days when the phone rang. It was my husband. He said, "Marie, I want you to come back to Omaha."

I said, "No way."

He said, "If you don't come back I'm going to kill the kids."

I was angry; I had been driven to the point of giving up. I said, "Ray, you're too far away, I can't stop you. If you want to kill them, kill them, because I am not coming back."

He said, "Then I'm going to kill them," and hung up.

Three hours later the phone rang and it was him again. I thought, "Oh no, he's going to torture me all night." It was about three in the morning.

He said, "I want you to be at the Greyhound bus depot day after tomorrow at midnight. Don't try to escape, because if you do, I'm going to beat the hell out of you."

So I went down to the bus depot. I walked all the way and it was a long walk. I got something to eat and went into a waiting area. Quite small. It was dreadfully late and I laid my head down on the arm piece, trying to rest. Something hit me on the head. I thought, "Oh my gosh, what was that?"

I looked up and there was a policeman with a billy club. He said, "Lady, you won't be loitering here."

I told him, "I'm not loitering. I'm waiting for my husband and daughters to come through the station."

He said, "That's a likely story. Get up and get out of here."

I said, "No, sir, because my husband told me to stay here and wait." He threatened me with a nudge of the billy club and I had to leave.

I went back home. I guess I slept for a couple hours when I heard a ruckus. Ray and the girls were there. I was surprised and overjoyed at the same time. I wanted nothing more than to hold my babies tight and never let them go. Ray laid across the middle of my bed and fell asleep. I'm not sure if he had been drinking. Me and my two daughters couldn't get into the bed. We stayed awake. Now that I had my two girls again, I began planning and scheming to get away.

### We're Sending You Back

We left that very night. From that time on, I traveled around with the girls. I kept in touch with my mother and sometimes my sister. I changed my name and social security number, but my husband always found me. I don't know how he found me. One time I think he actually did go to the social security board and threatened someone with a gun. I always feared for my life, for the life of my daughters.

As my pregnancy advanced, I eventually had to stop working. I went to the courthouse in San Diego and talked to a welfare worker there. She said, "We're sending you back to Nebraska." I told her I didn't want to go. She said, "You must, because you're not a resident here." I was becoming quite big with the baby. I must have been five or six months along.

While I was at the courthouse the welfare worker said, "Marie, I want you to pick up the extension over there. I'm calling Nebraska. I want you to listen to this. Hello—is this Nebraska? I'd like to talk to a person in charge of residents." We waited only five minutes and a man came to the telephone.

She continued, "We have a lady here with two little girls. One is three and the other one is two years old. We would like to have them returned to the state of Nebraska because they are your residents. The husband has abandoned the family. We want you to send money for their train fare and enough money for food so that they can get back to the state of Nebraska. The woman's name is Marie Grine."

The man at the other end of the line said, "Oh, we've had dealings with that woman before. We're not going to send you a solitary penny for the fare or for food."

She said, "I want you to know the state of California is not going to buy the ticket and pay for food on the way back. We'll take this case to the Supreme Court in order to find out who takes care of her."

The man said, "We'll send the money," and bang went the telephone. The money was wired in twelve minutes, and they sent twenty dollars too much. The welfare woman and I, we laughed our heads off. Nebraska had always been stingy, but the fact that my children were part Negro, that topped it. I always suspected the state welfare workers of being prejudiced.

## Saying Good-bye

When it came time to leave and go to the station my mother started acting peculiar. She walked from room to room, wringing her hands and sobbing. She threw her arms around my neck saying, "Oh, Marie, please don't go, please don't go."

I said, "Mother, I don't have any choice." I called a taxi-cab.

When the cab pulled up, I threw my arms around my mother and kissed her. I said, "Mother, I don't know how I'll ever get back out here, but I'll find some way to get back." I think my mother knew I would never see her again. I felt like I was losing my mother all over again.

I put my kids in the backseat of the taxi and climbed in, slamming the door. I wish I hadn't looked back. My mother was wailing, "Marie, don't go, don't take my babies away from me." She was running down the middle of the road. I felt hysterical, but then when I saw my kids' faces, I thought I better straighten up. Both my girls were crying. I told the driver to step on the gas.

At the train station where I bought my ticket, the man behind the counter said I could only take six hundred pounds, but there was more than that. My mother had given me so many boxes of things to take with me that they weren't even sealed shut properly. I believe my mother called a truck that picked up those boxes since they all made it with me to Omaha.

My welfare worker liked me; she even called me by my first name, which put me at ease. She was at the station to see me off. When we parted, there were tears in her eyes. She lifted my little girls onto the train and then took hold of my arm. She gave me the extra twenty dollar bill. She said, "I wish you the very best, Marie."

I was frightened beyond words. I knew terrible trouble was waiting for me back in Nebraska.

*One evening, I was rushing for the elevator in a typical hurry when I heard a shout behind me, "Sister, Sister! Please come and help me." I went over to the receptionist's desk to greet Marie and see how I might help. "Sister, see, I have some hot chicken soup here. It is for Senior Howard. He was telling me he just couldn't shake his cold. I just know it'll make him better." "Well, that's fine, Marie. I know he will love it." "No, no, Sister, wait, you don't understand. You have to tell this young man here that I'm OK to go up. He said he doesn't know me and can't let me by the desk." "She's fine to go on up to the floor," I said to the new brother at the desk. "She may not look it but she's really one of us," I said quietly to him as we watched her hurry to the elevator.*

—Katherine Williams

## The Train Back to Omaha

I'll never forget that ride. Even though I was sad to leave my mother because I loved her and even though I felt sorrow and grief going home, I'll never forget that ride.

Everybody in the United States should have a ride like I had. The train had glass in the top and you could see through it. I saw the sky and the clouds. We followed Highway 1, that ran along the coast. All the way I saw the ocean. There were boats on the water, fishermen, the Coast Guard, and mysterious huge birds. I don't know what they were. They had a wing span that seemed five or ten feet. Fish were jumping up in the air. That was a ride and a half. We were leaving San Diego and going to Los Angeles on the *Hiawatha*.

When we got to the Los Angeles station, it was made of white concrete or stone. All around were beautiful poinsettias; their huge stalks went straight up in the air. The stalks didn't have a solitary leaf on them, not even one. Then, all the sudden, there was a blossom about fifteen inches across. They were all along one side of the building.

We had a bit of a wait. I had the twenty dollar bill. So I went and bought the kids each a little celluloid doll because they didn't have anything to play with. Then we boarded the *Pony Express* heading back to Omaha. They sure didn't name this train right. If it wasn't jumping back and forth it was swaying from the left to the right. The baby inside of me kicked a lot, too. I was on that train for three days and three nights. I couldn't sleep.

We made it back to Omaha. I was five months pregnant. It was March 1948. First, we went to the Salvation Army where a woman treated us real bad. The food was horrible. We all vomited.

There was snow and slush on the ground. Me and the two girls were walking in this all day long trying to find a place to live, trying to go the courthouse, going to different places to get help. We went to the Red Cross, we went to the county, we went all over. But nobody would help us.

At the county courthouse they said, "You're not going to get any help here. We're calling the police."

I said, "That's just who I want to see."

But they didn't call the police. We were actually thrown out bodily. I told the kids, "Don't cry." Ellen said her feet were getting cold from walking in the slush. I said, "I'll take turns carrying you kids."

At one time I was carrying them both, one on my back, one in front. Carrying my shopping bag, purse, and everything. My legs were so numb from walking in that slush. I couldn't even feel my feet anymore. I came to Twenty-fourth and Cummings. Why I didn't pray, I don't know. I guess I was too scared to pray. I think I had a dollar and thirty-four cents in my pocket, something like that. And the thought went through my mind, "If there is a God above, He can see me walking with these children, and maybe He will help me."

I was walking in the slush with my children, I don't

remember what happened, but I found myself lying in the snow. The children were whining from the cold so I told them to lie on top of me. I don't remember what happened exactly, but a woman went by and called, "Ralph, there's a woman lying in the snow and she has children." I guess her husband didn't hear her, so she screamed it louder. She said, "Ralph, come quick and bring the flashlight."

Her husband came out and carried me. She carried the two little girls. They took us in the house and rubbed us with snow. We ended up living with Ralph and Lucille; she was the most marvelous person. They had six children and lived in a storefront partitioned off into rooms. Ralph's mother lived with them also. I helped take care of her kids. She had been wanting to go to work but couldn't find a babysitter. She treated my two little girls just like they were made out of gold.

I could talk a lot about Lucille and me and all the things I was able to accomplish in her home. All of the children, except her oldest one, wet the bed at night. She didn't know how to stop the bed-wetting. I had it stopped in three weeks. I was very proud of myself, but I was especially proud of the children. She had beautiful children. They lacked a lot of training in the home, but I realized I was being too strict with my children.

I remember sitting outside on a chair and every time my children's face and hands got dirty, I'd wipe them off. Lucille said, "My God, let those poor children play." Both of my two little girls were dreadfully thin when we arrived in Nebraska. One night Lucille had made a great big pot of beans with onion, bacon, and homemade bread. My kids were shoveling in the food just like her kids. I couldn't believe my eyes because my children were taking big spoonfuls which I usually forbid. Great big mouthfuls of bread, but they were happy. So I just let it go on like that.

My children had perfect manners. They could place their own orders in a restaurant. They were able to pay but couldn't count the change when they got it back. I remember one time when we were in a diner a woman said, "Oh, Marie, you're not going to let those children sit at the counter by themselves are you?" I said, "Sure." We were sitting at a booth where I could see them. My youngest one took the saltshaker and poured some salt on the counter. Ellen looked at her through the corner of her eye, a look which said, "If you don't clean that mess up I'll go get Mother." She put the salt in the ashtray and sat up there just like a little angel.

### Rose Moss

After living with Ralph and Lucille for a month or two, I got my own apartment upstairs. I contacted Ray and told him we were back in Omaha in hopes that we could live apart in peace. My little boy was buried west and north of my place in a beautiful cemetery. The lawn was always kept well cut. I was very happy the day we went to the cemetery. It was a beautiful day, a Sunday. I was dressed in a plain dress and my two little girls were wearing sundresses and little white ankle socks. They looked like two little dolls. I had about thirty packages of seeds and I planted rose moss all over his little grave. I felt my son watching me. I don't think it was in my imagination. It was so strange. I felt very close to him.

I was nearly due with my baby. It took me a minute to stand up from the grave side. We were just getting ready to leave when I saw my husband walking over the grass. My children yelled, "Daddy, Daddy," running to him. I never turned my children against their father. Perhaps I should have; they loved their father.

He came over to me, "I want sex out of you."

I said, "What? I can't do anything like that. First of all, I don't want sex out of you, and second, where would we go?"

He said, "Right here in the cemetery."

I said, "I think you have lost your mind. I think you're insane."

"If you don't lie down on the ground and have sex with me I'm going to call the police."

He called the police. I was standing on the sidewalk with my little rake and shovel. The police came over to me, "Did you beat this man up and pull a knife on him?"

I answered, "Heavens, no. I have been over here planting seed on my baby's grave. I've been planting rose moss." My husband began talking real fast so the police told him to shut his mouth.

The policeman asked me, "What seems to be the trouble?"

I said, "My husband wanted me to lie down and have sex with him on top of our son's grave."

The police put handcuffs on my husband and called for a patrol wagon. The paddy wagon looked exactly like the ones they carry the police dogs in. My daughters and I were waiting on the sidewalk when they put my husband in the wagon. Ellen, she said, "Ooky dat, Daddy's riding just like a doggy." Oh, I thought I would split. The people on the sidewalk just roared. I sure got a kick out of thinking about Ray riding in a dogcatcher's wagon.

### Peace Not Possible

Sometime later it was my husband's birthday. I had taken the last penny that I had and bought a present for him, some Old Spice shaving lotion and a bottle of talcum. I bought the best they had in the drugstore. I left the store and began walking down the street. I had my two little girls by the hands when Ray came up to me on the sidewalk. "I want you to come up to my sister's house and have sex with me."

I said, "No. I will never have sex again." Then to show I wasn't completely mad at him I said, "I bought a birthday present for you."

He asked, "Why did you do that? You told me you don't love me anymore."

I said, "Ray, I don't love you anymore. I don't think I ever did love you. It was infatuation because I was afraid to live alone."

I had taken great pains wrapping the present up in tissue paper. I had my girls sign a birthday card. He was so furious that he hit the birthday package. It landed on the sidewalk and both the bottles broke. The powder and the after-shave cologne mixed together all over the sidewalk. He said, "If you don't come up to Pearl's house to have sex with me, you're going to be sorry."

Ray grabbed a hold of Ellen's hand and pulled her loose from me. He lost hold of her and she landed in the street. I panicked. There was a car coming real fast, a great big Cadillac. The driver, his face was as white as death, put on the brakes. He was trying to stop his car. He couldn't swerve because the street was narrow. By instinct I ran into the street and grabbed my daughter's dress—that's all I had a chance to get hold of. The squealing car tire missed her by inches. When I dragged her past the curb I banged her head; I was so frightened and scared. Ellen began screaming with the pain, then she screamed at her father. She was afraid of her father after that.

I decided that very moment that a peaceful existence with this man was just not possible. I decided to get out of Omaha. Just a few hours before leaving I went to the grocery store. I was walking home with a sack of groceries. Again I ran right into my husband. He looked very strange. I don't think he'd been drinking beer, but his eyes were swimming around inside his head. He was really talking like a crazy person.

He said, "Come with me."

"No. Ray, I'm not going with you."

"Well, I'm taking the children with me."

I said, "You're not going to take the children with you."

"You stay right here," he said. "I'll be back." The look on his face told me he was going to kill me and the children.

I set my groceries up on a great big incinerator and grabbed my two kids. We ran as fast as we could down the sidewalk. Ellen said, "Oh, Mama, my foot." I looked down and asked her, "Do you love me?" She answered, "Mama, you know I love you." I said, "Well, honey, you run, hear me?" I'll never forget that little kid. She said, "Oh, Mommy, it hurts, I love you, it hurts, I run Mommy, I run, I run fast, that's how much I love you." I prayed, "God help us."

I turned to the right. There was an old garage which didn't have a roof. It only had one wall; the other three walls had collapsed. I climbed in there with my kids. There was an old car seat there and that's where I laid Lilith down. She fell asleep after awhile. She slept through the whole thing, but Ellen didn't. She started screaming. I put my hand over her mouth and looked through a crack in the garage.

I could have touched my husband's pant leg with my forefinger, that's how close he was. In the moonlight I saw that he had a great big piece of steel pipe. He hollered in the darkness, "Marie, I'm going to kill you, but before I kill you I'm going to kill both of your kids in front of your eyes. Then I'm going to kill you." He was swinging that pipe over his head. I was so scared I thought my heart was going to quit. Then Ellen's body went limp.

I thought he was never going to walk away. Finally, he took the pipe and threw it. He said, "That's all right. I'll catch you someday and when I do, I'm going to kill you."

After he left I carried Ellen to a streetlight because I couldn't see very well. She was limp; I thought she was dead. I touched her heart, and it was beating, but beating awfully slow. I carried her home and laid her on the bed, then I thought, "Oh my gosh, I have another baby in the garage! I've got to go back and get Lilith." I went back to the garage and got Lilith and put her on the other side of the bed. She was still asleep. I got on my knees and prayed for Ellen. "Oh, God, I lost one baby. Please don't let this one die, too."

I didn't know how to trust God at that time. My prayers were like banging my head on a stone wall. I needed God so bad, but I didn't know how to reach him.

I got up and went to the window to look out. I heard a noise and turned around. Ellen was up on her elbow. "Mommy, I waked up." I grabbed that little girl off the bed and hugged her so tight.

### Streetcar Out of Omaha

It was a dreadfully hot day. I went downstairs and told Lucille, "I gotta get out of here quick. My baby is due any day. I can tell. My baby's starting to quiver."

Someone had hooked up a hose in the street so that water sprayed out into the air. I held Lilith in my arms and took my big girl by the hand and went outside. We were dancing and jumping around in the spray.

My insurance man came walking up. He was a wonderful man. He said, "Mrs. Grine." I said, "Oh my goodness, I don't want you to see me all wet like this." I was wearing a cotton dress that had a beautiful white collar and a great big skirt so you couldn't see my stomach. I was a sight.

He asked me, "Do you still have your insurance policy?" I said, "Yes, I do, but it has run out. I haven't been on my insurance for two years. It's not any good anymore."

He said, "If you make the back payments, the insurance would still be good."

I said, "I can't do that. I can't even feed myself. We're eating hard cinnamon rolls three times a day. No milk."

He said, "Did you know that you can draw hundreds of dollars on that insurance policy?"

I went upstairs, got my policy out of my shoe box, and handed it to him. My hair was dripping wet. He said, "You can borrow about three hundred dollars. You'll get it immediately, as soon as you ask for it, but take your policy with you."

Next morning I asked Lucille to watch the kids. "I'm going to walk all the way downtown and all the way back. I'm going to see if I can get this money." I went downtown and got $304. All I had to do was ask for it and sign the papers. I had quite a bit of stuff in storage. I went down to the storage place and paid that, and they brought the stuff and put it in Lucille's house.

I didn't know what to do to escape because Ray would

be watching the airport and Greyhound station. I had my stuff all packed and ready to go. Just then a streetcar went by. It was hot and paper was flying up in the air. All that dust and everything. I said, "That's it. I'll take a streetcar across the river. They're not going to be watching at Council Bluffs, Iowa. They're going to be watching in Omaha. I'll go to Council Bluffs.

Three o'clock in the morning I woke my kids up. I had put them to bed with all their clothes on, except their shoes. I said, "Ellen, wake up."

"Mommy?"

I said, "Honey, are you awake?"

"I think so."

I said, "Honey, you're not awake very good. Let Mommy wash your face with this cold washcloth." When I touched her with the washcloth she jumped. "It's all right. I just have to make sure you're awake. How old are you?"

"Mommy, I three."

"Honey, I'm gonna take these two suitcases down. I'm gonna put them on the corner where we catch the streetcar. Will you do something for Mommy? Will you stand there and keep your hands on the suitcases until Mommy gets back?" She frowned. "Don't talk to nobody."

I dashed across that street, ran up those steps, and grabbed my purse, shopping bag, and little Lilith. We hopped on the streetcar. I left Omaha that night and went to Council Bluffs, Iowa, and then eventually came to Chicago, Illinois.

That was my first time in Chicago. We walked the streets for a day and a half. We had no food, no place to sleep. We went to the park. I sat on the park bench and prayed. "God, you know I'm pregnant and have two little girls. We need food. Please supply food." I opened my eyes and saw a man with a popcorn machine. He was dumping popcorn out onto the ground. There was a five foot circle of popcorn. We dived into the popcorn on our bellies. We ate popcorn till it was coming out of our ears.

We wound up at the Salvation Army. A woman there said, "Mrs. Grine, you've been here two days. We're going to watch the children while you go down to Cook County Hospital. You are to be examined. Then when you come back we are going to put you on a Greyhound bus and you are going to leave Chicago immediately. Leave the state."

I said, "I'm ready to give birth." She said, "You're not big enough to birth a mouse." I said, "You might think so, but my baby is going to be born tonight." She said, "How can you be sure?" I said, "Because of the quivering."

I went to Cook County Hospital where the doctor said to me, "Lady, did you know you're already in labor?" I was put into a ward. There was a black woman moaning next to me. I tried talking to her.

"Are you in a lot of pain?"

"Yes, ma'am." She said.

"I wish there was something I could do for you." She was all by herself. It was dreadful hot, the twenty-fifth of

July. I said, "You're perspiring so bad. There's a pitcher of water by your bed and some Kleenex. If I wet this with some ice cold water and put that on your forehead will that make you feel better?"

She said, "Oh, yes." I put that on her forehead and she smiled.

Growing up I was always told there was a difference between black and white people. I didn't believe it. I told this woman we were sisters. "We're both pregnant, we're both in labor. That makes us the same." How could my parents teach me what they did? That was wrong.

I talked to her while I waited for my baby to be born. All of a sudden she begged the doctor, "Please do something." She was in a lot of pain, but the doctors and nurses didn't do anything to help her. She asked me, "Do you hear the bells?"

I lied, "Yes."

She said, "Isn't it pretty? Oh, listen Marie." I looked over and she was dead.

Soon after that I was wheeled into the delivery room. The doctor asked me, "Have you ever given birth without any ether gas?" I answered, "No, sir." The nurse said, "The baby's head is ready to be born. What sort of feeling do you have?" I said, "It quivers about every half minute. Trembling."

I had never seen or had any experience quite like what happened to me at Cook County. My feet were up high in the stirrups, my knees were up by my ears, and I was pushing as hard as I could.

"Push!" I pushed, but it hurt and I quit. I had two interns and they said, "Oh, Mrs. Grine, you can't quit. Your baby is waiting to be born. You can't quit."

I began pushing again and screaming bloody murder. Then they put my knees down. They took my feet out of the stirrups.

I felt something between my legs. I said, "Doc, you made me strain so hard that my guts are coming out."

The doctor patted me on the knee. He said, "Mrs. Grine, that wasn't your guts." The baby's head gushed out. "Hold real still," the doctor said, "because we don't want any brain damage. Hold your legs real still. Rest, because we have a tough one ahead of us."

They put my knees up again, hooked my feet back in the stirrups, and I started to push again. I was exhausted and wanted to stop. The head doctor came over, "Mrs. Grine, do you want your baby born dead or alive?" He was spitting in my face. For a moment I thought I was in the lumber wagon with my dad. He said, "Hold on, Marie." I held on to the side of the wagon. I fell over backwards because I couldn't hold on any longer. Dad said, "Hold on." I said, "Okay, doc, I'm ready to go. Let her fly."

I screamed and heard, "Waaah!" I sat up. To this day I don't know what was happening during that odd delivery, but my baby was cute. Cute, fat, and mad.

The doctor told me to lie back down; I was losing a lot of blood. All the time I was giving birth I heard church bells. I thought I was dying. So, I asked the nurse, "I'm dying, aren't I?"

"Oh, no," she said, "you're fit as a fiddle. You're one of the strongest women we've had in here."

I said, "I can hear church bells. That's why I think I'm dying."

She said, "I can hear them, too. Mrs. Grine, it's Sunday morning in Chicago."

I named my son Victor because he was a victory over his brother's death. Victor Norman. That's what they put on the birth certificate.

### Leaving Chicago

I was rolled back to the ward. I felt woozy, but I wanted to hold my baby so bad. I asked the girl in the next bed, "How long do we have to wait for bedpans?" She said, "They don't bring any bedpans." I got out of bed, put my feet on the floor, and felt something like needles in my feet. I had to hang on to the bed and the wall to get to the bathroom and back. Immediately I was told I could leave the hospital and go home. With my other births, I usually stayed in the hospital for a week.

I looked a mess. I was hemorrhaging, milk was coming out of my breasts, and I was sore from top to toe. I had on an expensive dress that couldn't be washed, it had to be dry cleaned, and it was getting ruined. I went downstairs and there stood my husband.

When we were leaving the hospital after baby Victor's birth a social worker asked me where I had been staying. I said, "Salvation Army." She told my husband and me to get in the van. While we were riding to the Salvation Army she said, "You've got twenty-four hours to get out of Chicago or you'll both be put in jail and your baby will be taken away." We had to do some fast thinking.

When we got to the Salvation Army building I laid my baby down in front of the woman who had said you aren't big enough to have a mouse. My baby weighed nine pounds. I laid him right down on her desk and said, "Here's my nine-pound mouse."

I was skin and bones, but my baby was healthy. He started to cry. I told my husband I had to go upstairs because my baby was wet. I went upstairs and put some dry pants on him. He still cried so I started nursing. I was getting milk from my breasts. My beautiful dress was soaked with milk.

My husband stepped to the doorway. He was jealous. He said, "You shouldn't be holding that baby. You should be holding me." I said, "What are you talking about? The baby is hungry." He said, "Well, you could put it in bed and prop a bottle up to his mouth." I said, "Ray, you're jealous."

Victor was a good baby. Beautiful. I told Ray we had to go get the girls. They were in a holding home. "I want those girls. Right away." He said, "I don't know where to go. Chicago scares me." He acted like he didn't want to go, but he finally did.

He brought back the girls, but no clothes. I was angry. "What is wrong with you? Why didn't you bring their clothes?" I had to go all the way back with the two little girls because I was afraid of what he would do next. I had the two little girls, my baby, my purse, a shopping bag with diapers, and then I had to go get two big suitcases. We finally ended up at the Greyhound bus depot.

A woman at the station asked, "How old is your baby?" I said, "Four hours old." The police came and said, "Your baby is four hours old and you are out of the hospital?" I told them I was not from Illinois and we had to leave.

My husband asked, "Where should we go?" I said, "Milwaukee, that's the biggest town nearby." My husband didn't want to go up there. I said, "We don't have any choice. It's only ninety-seven miles and we have to get out of here right away."

### Milwaukee

When we got to Milwaukee we found a small room where the baby slept in an orange crate. I nursed Victor for three weeks. I noticed a place on my breast was starting to get red. I became frightened. The milk was getting less and less. We had no money for formula. I told this woman we rented from, "I'm getting less and less milk all the time and there's a big red spot on my breast." She asked if I would be embarrassed if she looked at it. I told her no.

She said, "Marie, you have an infection." She called the doctor. "You have to stop nursing."

I had to start feeding the baby from a bottle so I got a good job. I was making two hundred dollars a week and on the weekends I waitressed. I found a woman with children of her own who would take care of the baby and my two little girls. I paid her fifteen dollars a week. I had a good job.

My husband wouldn't work. I gave him five dollars a day until one day I saw him come out of a bar and walk down the street with a girl on each arm. That was the last time I gave him any money. I knew my husband was messing around with other women. One time after intercourse, as he was pulling out, he told me, "Marie, do you know how many places this has been in?" I said, "No, Ray." "Well, if I can't get it from you, Marie, I get it from other women, and if I can't get it from other women, I get it from other men." I understood what Ray meant. I felt the blood drain from my body. After that I started taking baths and douches. I was afraid I'd catch a disease from my husband.

Ray was getting more and more dangerous. He used to pull a gun on me all the time. One day he took me to some people's apartment. I didn't want to go. I didn't like the looks of the place. My husband went into a side room and talked with some other men in low tones. They were either planning a robbery job or my husband was trying to get money from this guy. The wife invited me into the kitchen for coffee and sandwiches, but I wouldn't go because I was afraid.

One day I came home from work and went to pick up my kids, which I did every night. My kids and both suitcases were gone. My husband took the kids; I didn't know where they were. My baby was eight weeks old. I went numb and cried until there were no tears left in my body. Then it was dry agony. I felt like a stick walking around.

I didn't see my kids for a whole year. I did a lot of things that year that I was ashamed of. I was a confused person. I had the loss of my kids and my memories to torment me. I rented a different place and gave my old landlady the phone number to my new place in case Ray called or came back. I dated married men and even had sex with one of them. I was lonely and afraid. Life didn't have any meaning; I didn't feel like a mother. I thought I couldn't live without my babies.

One day about a year later I was living in the suburbs in a rich neighborhood when the buzzer rang and the landlady came in. She said, "There's a man outside the door that says he's your husband." I ran to the door and got a gun pointed at me. He said, "Get out here." I stepped outside. He said, "You're coming back with me." I said, "Ray, give me a chance to get my coat and purse." He said, "You're coming with me right now." I was afraid he was going to shoot me right on that woman's porch. I think he would have. I was twenty-three years old.

### Forced Back to Omaha

He took me back to Omaha with a gun, all the way on a Greyhound bus. After we got back there terrible things happened. He took me way out on the west part of town where his brother Henry and his wife had the kids. When I saw my kids I thought my heart was going to quit. My baby was walking. My oldest girl was standing in the middle of the floor. When she saw me she didn't move a muscle, but tears were going down her face like a river. She screamed, "Mommy, Mommy."

Then we went to his sister Ruth's house. She and her boyfriend got into an argument and she threw a knife which just missed my smallest girl's head. I told Ray, "Get us out of here tonight. If you don't I'm going to take these two girls and start walking the streets. I'm not going to stay here with those knives flying around the room."

He found another place for us to go that same night. It was one room hooked to a filling station. One room and one bed with a big blood spot on the bed. I said, "Some lady must have had a bad monthly. Help me turn the mattress over." We didn't have any blankets. I kept a hitting stick by me all night to scare the rats because they were so bad.

The next day my husband went out to look for work. I was out shoveling snow. A black man started talking to me. He asked, "You renting that little room?" I said, "Yeah." He said, "I didn't think anyone would rent that place after that woman was murdered in her bed." I dropped the snow shovel and headed back to the shack for my kids.

I rented another place in a private home, a large room in a house owned by a lady named Virginia. I had to live with my husband and let him have sex with me. Sex wasn't any fun for me, but I thought, well, maybe if I pleased him then maybe the beatings would stop. Soon I got tired of the beatings; I got tired of his mouth.

### I Almost Killed Him

One night we had an argument. He pulled out his gun again. I said, "Ray, I am so tired of you pointing that gun at me. Go ahead and shoot me. Get it over with. I am tired of pulling these kids one way and then another, chasing all over the country trying to find them and you. I've had it. I love my kids, but every time I turn around you take them away from me. You don't want them. You dangle them in front of my nose and use them for bait. I want you to shoot me."

He threw the gun on the sofa. I cracked the gun open and there wasn't one shell in it. After all that, after all the fear, he was nothing but a lot of hot air. His words had no meaning.

After that Ray didn't live with me at Virginia's place, but he did keep some of his things there. He kept a drawer full of his clothes and other personal effects like a fountain pen. I don't remember if I got a restraining order on him or what, but I know he had to get permission to come and see me.

My husband never spoke to Victor from the day he was born. Never held him or nothing. Victor had great big yellow curls all over his head and great big brown eyes. He was fat and, oh, he was cute. One day my husband was all dressed up, white shirt and necktie. My little boy was creeping on the floor. He said, "Dada, Dada." He held his arms up to Ray. Ray said, "Get away from me you filthy rotten little pig."

I said, "Ray, he's been creeping. He wants you to hold him."

He said, "I ain't holding that bastard." Victor cried and cried because his daddy wouldn't hold him. I went over and picked the baby up. I told Ray, "Someday you're going to pay for this."

Once, I almost killed him. On purpose. He was lying on the sofa on his belly, and I had a knife. I thought how easy it would be to stick it in him. I don't know what stopped me.

Ray would torment me by saying that God took Douglas because I was unfaithful. I was absolutely dumbfounded. One day I was sitting by the piano in a chair. Ray was sitting in an armchair about two feet from me. He said, "Marie, there is something I've got to tell you. Please don't look at me because if you do I'm going to lose my nerve. I won't be able to tell you; please look at the floor. Do you remember the day little baby Douglas died?"

"Yes."

"Marie," his voice trembled, "I beat Douglas real, real bad. I went in twenty minutes later and he was dead. I killed him."

It was all over. I never saw Ray again.

## The Detectives

I came home from work one night to find Virginia sitting on the porch. She said, "Marie, did you see the paper?" I said, "No." She said, "Your husband is right on the front page." Ray had committed a robbery.

Three days later I got a letter from Mexico. It read, "Please come out here. I want you to be with me." It was from Ray. I didn't even answer it; I didn't want to see him and I didn't want to be with him.

Then a couple of detectives started in on me. They almost drove me crazy. Every night they'd be waiting for me. I got off work at two-thirty in the morning. I had to walk quite a ways to the viaduct. Then I had to go up a hill. I had taken off my high heel shoes and nylons and I was walking barefoot because my feet hurt. I was walking north and had a funny feeling that someone was watching me. My skin was crawling. I looked all around and didn't see anybody, but I could feel eyes watching me.

I saw a squad car parked in the alley; it was sitting right on the sidewalk. The hind end of the squad car was hanging half into the street. I went to walk around the back of the squad car and the policeman said, "Get in the car." I asked, "What for?" He said again, "Get in the car."

These same two policemen had been bothering me all night long at the restaurant. The Italian one said they were going to take me out to Carter Lake. I was so scared they were going to rape me. I couldn't even pray. I thought, "Well, if I'm going to die, I'm going to try to save myself."

We came to a red light. I started screaming bloody murder just as loud as I could scream. The policeman that was driving had just turned the corner. They stopped the car and kicked me out.

I landed right on the middle line of the pavement. They took off. I fell right on my chin and belly. I remember watching my lipstick roll to the curb when my purse had flown open. I was hurting so bad I couldn't get up. I don't know how long I laid there. Cars were going by on both sides; nobody stopped. I guess they thought I was drunk.

An old man came up to me and said, "Lady, are you all right?" I said, "No, I'm hurting." He asked, "Do you want me to call the police?" I said, "Heavens no."

### Where's the Gun?

I never went back to the restaurant to work anymore. The police would come to my job and say terrible things to insult me. It was all because of Ray. They were looking for Ray.

Another night I came home and this time detectives were there waiting on the sofa. My two little girls were there and my baby was crawling along the floor. I said, "Are you guys here again? What in the world for this time?"

They said, "Where's the gun?"

I said, "I told you a million times I do not know where the gun is. I don't have the slightest idea."

"Your husband told us that it is in the shape of a fountain pen and is in the third drawer from the top."

I went and got what I thought was a fountain pen from his drawer.

The one detective said, "This is a gun all right." I had no way of knowing. It looked like a fountain pen to me, but it had a hole in the end. He asked, "Mrs. Grine, where's your husband? Usually a husband tries to contact his wife some kind of way. He should have called you on the telephone or wrote a letter or something."

I didn't say anything. He had written a letter four days before that. Somehow the detectives knew about the letter and told me to go get it. I refused. I was afraid if Ray found out he would kill me. He would kill me even from prison once he was caught. There was no way I could put him away. I told the police it wasn't my job to hunt for him. My husband married me when I was pregnant. He supported these kids for six and a half years. "He's still my husband and he is very much the father of my children. I'm not going to squeal on him. I'm not going to uphold him when he's wrong, but I'm not going to turn him in either. Now I expect you to find him and arrest him." They didn't like the sound of my words.

Lilith, who was two years old, saw the cute little gun lying on the cocktail table. My little girl walked over there and picked up the gun and had it pointed to her face. She said, "Oh, Mama, look at that! It got a hole."

I died a thousand deaths. I was shaking from head to foot. I am shaking right now just thinking about it. I calmly took the gun out of her hands. One of the detectives said,

"You wouldn't want anything to happen to one of your little girls would you? Why would you protect a man that puts your children in danger? Go get that letter."

I went and got the letter: it was underneath the diapers. I handed it to him. They didn't even bother to take the steps; they jumped right over the side of the porch. Both of them. Hopped in the car and they were gone. Ray went to prison; he got one to twenty years. I didn't even watch him get sentenced. I was sick of the whole mess.

※ ※ ※

I tried to get assistance for my three children. We were very poor. A welfare woman kept heckling me. She said, "Mrs. Grine, I don't believe that that baby with the blonde curls is your husband's son. How can that baby have yellow hair when your husband is half Negro?"

I said, "He is one-fourth Irish."

She said, "I think that you're making up this story to cover up the fact that you got pregnant by some other man." She made me come down to the courthouse and get a blood test. I said, "You can have as much blood as you want."

Four days later I went down and they took blood out of my arm. I heard a story that they went to Lincoln, Nebraska, to take blood from my husband. When they went in to get blood out of my husband's arm, and I don't know if they did because he was afraid of the needle, but they said he was standing up. He put his arm up against the wall of the prison and leaned on it. He started sobbing just like a baby. They said, "What are you crying about?" He said, "That little boy with the yellow hair is my son." They asked, "Why then have you denied him all these years?" He said, "Just to torment my wife."

I never saw my husband when he was on parole or when he got out. I never laid eyes on him again.

*The first time I met Marie I was hurrying through the lobby. Someone called out, "Rebecca!" and I stopped to talk. Marie said, "Oh Sister, Sister, is your name Rebecca?" I said yes, and her eyes filled with tears. "That's my daughter's name," she said. "I haven't seen her in years and years."*

*Marie wanted me to get married. I didn't even have a boyfriend, so she decided to take matters into her own hands. We'd be sitting at a picnic table in the yard and a brother would walk by. She would yell, "Oh, Brother, don't you think Rebecca has pretty hair?" The poor guy would mumble something and hurry off, and I would hiss under my breath, "Marieeee!"*

*Once on the way home from one of our frequent emergency midnight runs for this or that we stopped to get gas. I was pumping the gas, and when I turned around she wasn't in the car. I looked over to the booth and Marie was talking to the turban-clad gentleman inside. As I approached, I heard her saying, "And she's a very sweet girl. She'd make any man a wonderful wife. Don't you think she's pretty?" The guy looked up and gave me a sickly gold-toothed smile. "Marie!!!" I couldn't believe it. "Get in the car!"*

—Rebecca Hill

## I Wasn't an Unfit Mother

I couldn't get any help for my kids. One of my little girls got sick and had to go to the hospital for malnutrition. Instead of letting me know when it was time for my little girl to come home, they just placed her in a home north of where I lived. They came and got my other little girl and the baby and took them both to a home. Ellen was about five. Lilith was three. My baby was one. The welfare workers said I was an unfit mother.

Every time I went to visit my children at the home I started crying. My two daughters would be crying; my son didn't cry. My oldest one especially cried something terrible. I went to see the kids several times, but the woman told me I couldn't come back and see them anymore.

This was a very sad period in my life.

That's when I drank Lysol. It was a small bottle and only half full. My tongue swelled up until it was two and a half inches thick. The insides of my mouth were raw, like sand paper. I didn't go to the hospital, though. A woman I was living with helped me by keeping me alive. At first I couldn't swallow water, but finally, I got to where I could talk and drink liquids. I sipped soup through a straw, then cream of wheat mixed with a lot of milk. I couldn't taste anything for over a year.

I tried to commit suicide several times after that first incident. I jumped in the river; I jumped in front of a semi truck. My kids had been my whole world. I never had anything to love, nobody had ever loved me. The only thing I had was my kids . . . and now they were gone.

During this time I couldn't hold a job or keep an apartment. I climbed into cars with people I didn't know, just to have someone to talk to. I went to bars to get drunk. I drank to get drunk but only managed to get sick; there was no escape from my misery. I thought I was losing my mind.

### Gail

I went to the same bar for a couple of weeks where I met a man. He was sitting with a lady in a booth and he was very attractive. I was sitting alone at the bar. I didn't look very good at the time. He walked over to me and said, "Excuse me, my name is Gail. Would you care to dance?"

"Yes, I would, but nobody has asked me."

He asked me my name. "Marie, would you like to dance with me?"

"I don't know if I should dance with you. Your lady friend in the booth might get angry or jealous."

He laughed, "That's my sister." We began to dance.

That was the beginning of a strange relationship between Gail and myself. We became very good friends. I dated him for a long time, maybe three months. Finally, one night he kissed me goodnight. I almost fainted. He kissed me on the cheek. I was used to dating men that would at least kiss me on the lips. He just kissed me on the cheek, squeezed my hand, and said goodnight. It must have been a month after the first kiss that he finally kissed me on the lips. It wasn't much of a kiss. Sort of like someone tapping their fingers lightly on a tabletop and then he was gone. Gail was a difficult person to understand.

He came over to my apartment one day. "I gotta get out."

"Why?" I asked.

He said, "Never mind, just come with me." We went over to a restaurant. "Marie, I gotta get out of town. I set my hotel room on fire. I got drunk and must have let a cigarette burn a hole in the bed and set the room on fire." In Omaha, they have a law. You get thirty days in jail and a fifty-dollar fine for setting a hotel room on fire.

We hitchhiked up to Milwaukee. This was the first time I had ever hitchhiked. While trying to get a ride, we had to walk across a bridge over the Missouri River. When we were crossing the river I looked down. I said, "Someone told me that if you throw a pebble in the river and make a wish before it hits the water, your wish will come true."

He said, "You don't believe that do you?"

"Sure." I couldn't find a pebble on the bridge, but I had some mints in my purse. "I will do it with a breath mint." So I pulled out a white mint and dropped it in the water.

I wished that I would have a baby girl. I didn't want to go through another pregnancy and labor; I was rather hoping that I could find someone who had a baby girl that didn't want her. I was going to take her and run as far and as fast as I could. I told Gail that I wished that I would have a baby girl.

He started laughing. Gail laughed more than any other man I knew. Most of my boyfriends were sad or very serious. I asked him, "Why don't you make a wish?"

He said, "I am going to." He dropped a breath mint into the water. "I'm not going to tell mine."

"Well, then it might not come true."

He turned as red as a beet. He wished that I would marry him.

My relationship with Gail was very strange. We were like brother and sister. It was the first time I ever spent much time with a man without a lot of kissing or making sex.

We had a wonderful trip. We rode with some beautiful people such as a man who kept horses. He took us to his stable which was very exciting. He let me pet the horses and talk to them. Whenever I saw a horse I ached inside. I still missed my horse from when I was growing up on the farm.

When we arrived in Milwaukee we had six dollars and fifty cents between us. There was a police officer standing in the middle of the street. He was directing traffic. I waited till the traffic went by so I wouldn't get run over. I went up to him, "Excuse me sir, I just hit town and I don't have very much money. I don't have a job and I'm looking for a place to live."

He said, "Right across the street is the Black's Hotel."

So Gail and I went there. We registered as man and wife. I did that because we were short on cash. I think the manager suspected we weren't married. He never asked to see a marriage certificate. Nevertheless, I felt uncomfortable. I wished we were married because I wanted another baby.

I wanted to have sex right away and have a baby, but Gail wanted to wait. We slept in the same bed, but he didn't touch me that way. I tried to be patient. I remembered my father saying to me, "Marie, a women's virtue is like an empty seashell once it is gone, it's gone forever." My conscience bothered me a little even though I was no longer a virgin.

Gail and I used to go walking in the evenings. We would always go to a small restaurant for our supper. French and Irish. Quaint and clean. The proprietor was a swell fellow. We had the same thing every night: a bowl of chili, a glass of milk, and a piece of pie. Gail drank beer instead of milk. We used to stay awake until two or three in the morning just talking. Gail was sort of dreamy.

Once we looked in a pet store window and saw two white mice. He said, "I love those white mice." He wanted to buy the mice, but I was deathly afraid of them. I said, "Not in my room." He said, "Look at all those tricks they can do. They can make that wheel go around."

He bought them. On Saturdays the maids came to clean the room and leave fresh towels. I asked him, "Did you put those mice away?" He said, "I think I did. I put them in the closet in the shoe box with the door shut." We were planning to leave the room and were all the way across the hallway when I heard screaming. Gail had forgotten to put the mice away. I heard the maid remark, "I'm not going to clean that room no more."

One evening Gail and I were sitting on the edge of the bed, talking. I told him again that I wanted a baby girl.

He said, "I will make you pregnant."

I said, "Oh, Gail, come on, you've only kissed me twice. We haven't even had sex."

"Marie, you try to rush things."

"Maybe I do, but I don't want to wait forever." It was the first time I ever asked a man for sex. I was so embarrassed, I could have jumped into a hole in the floor.

Gail had a plan. "Let's wait three weeks."

"Three weeks! I want it now."

"Go place a mark on the calendar, Marie. Drink lots of milk, take walks in the sunshine. Get fresh air and learn to relax." We began to take more walks, either around the block or to the park to sit on a park bench eating popcorn.

We'd row a boat down the river. After three weeks I had relaxed to the point where I didn't feel like having sex. He said, "I don't either. Let's wait another three weeks."

Things changed one day. We still lived at Black's Hotel where there was one large shower room shared by all the residents, men and women. The door was kept closed, but not locked. We had a system worked out so that no one would be embarrassed. I'd stick my head in the door and ask, "Is it a gentleman or a lady?" If the answer was "a lady," well, then I'd go in. If it was a gentleman I'd say, "That's okay, I'll wait."

Well, one night Gail got home before I did. I had a job; it didn't pay too much, but it was a nice job. I put my robe over my arm, I had my towel and soap, and headed down the hall to the shower. I stuck my head in the door and I asked, "Is it a lady or a gentleman?" Nobody answered, but I could hear the water running, you know. I stood there for a couple of seconds. Then I saw Gail without a stitch of clothes. It was then I began to doubt if he could actually make me pregnant. I began to laugh. I said, "Why Gail, you couldn't make a fly pregnant with that little bitty thing you have." He was really angry with me for saying that.

We had sex twice after that, and both times I reached a climax. I was surprised, because with my husband that never happened. I hated sex with my husband because there was always so much pain. I always thought sex was supposed to make you happy, but with Ray I'd say, "Hurry up and get it over with." Gail was different. He asked me a lot of questions about how I felt and how he could make me happy. He asked me questions about Ray. "What kind of man was your husband?" I said, "He didn't care if I had any feeling or not." He said, "That's terrible. You must've gone through a terrible ordeal."

Four nights later we came home from the chili place and the next morning I vomited green. He asked, "What's the matter with you?"

I answered, "I'm pregnant."

Gail picked me up and took me out onto the fire escape. He shouted to our neighbors, "We're going to have a baby!"

I was so embarrassed. I said, "Put me down. Everybody's looking at us."

"That's what I want them to do!" He was really excited.

### I Didn't Love Gail

When I found out I was pregnant I went numb. Gail began to change, or maybe it was me. He wasn't exactly the kind of man I was looking for, to support me and all. I would have married him just to keep from being lonely. I bickered with him about little things. One day I was too sick to go to work. Gail fixed me breakfast. He stirred some raw oatmeal into a pan of lukewarm water and gave it to me. It was still crunchy.

I tried to hold my tongue. "Gail, is this all you're giving me for breakfast?"

"That's all I can find." He paused a minute, "I bought a car."

I asked, "Why? What for?"

"I'm going to Traverse City, Michigan, to see my mother. She's starting to get old." Then as an afterthought he added, "I'm taking her over six hundred dollars."

I was furious. "What about me, the baby?"

He said, "I want my mother to have the money."

"I'm not asking for all of it, but I'm not going to be able to work very much longer. The baby is going to need shirts and diapers."

He didn't say too much. He kissed me on the forehead and walked out the door. He didn't slam the door, but said quietly, "I'll be back."

I called out, "When you come back I won't be here." He kept going.

I jumped out of bed. I was in a rage. I began throwing clothes all around that room, toothbrushes, toothpaste. I even threw my electric iron at the wall. I took that oatmeal and gave it to the birds. I pulled my suitcases out of the closet and packed them both, everything I had. I didn't love Gail. I guess that's why I didn't cry.

The next thing I did was buy a newspaper. I began looking for a new apartment. I found one not too far from where I was, so I walked up there and asked if the apartment was for rent. It was. The manager took me upstairs to look at the room. It had hot water, good ventilation, and the toilet worked. I rented it.

One day there was a knock at the door of my new apartment. It was Gail, the last person on earth I wanted to see.

I didn't want a man around; I just wanted my baby. I stood there looking at him.

"Aren't you going to ask me in?"

"I guess so, but I don't care if you go or stay."

"Do you really mean that?" he asked.

I said, "I certainly do."

"Why are you acting like this?"

"Because you and I have put ourselves in the shoes of a married couple. We're going to have a child. It needs support. Not just a mother, it needs a father too. If you don't want to be a father to it, that's fine; I'll find some way to raise the baby and take care of it."

He said, "I want you and I want the baby."

At the time he came in I was just getting ready to start breakfast. I was going to have cold cereal, toast, and orange juice. When Gail came, I said, "A couple slices of toast isn't going to hold you. I better make a stack of pancakes and some bacon." I opened the cupboard and there was no syrup. I had already stirred up the batter and had the skillet going and the coffee was perking. I asked Gail to run quick to the store and bring back a bottle of syrup.

He came back an hour later with a teeny tiny bottle of syrup. He handed it to me and threw it right back at him. I said, "What do you think I'm going to do with a little dab of syrup?" He said, "I only had nineteen cents."

I told him to get out of my sight. "You said you gave your mother over six hundred dollars while me and the baby are going to starve to death. Why didn't you give her part of the money and part of it to me? Then everything would have been just fine. I wouldn't resent you sending money to your mother. I'd be happy if you did it, but don't let us starve."

He fell on his knees. "Marie, I love you and I want you to marry me."

I said, "I wouldn't marry you if you were the last man on earth." I took my foot and pushed him over backwards. I was furious. He walked out the door and I haven't seen him since. I hollered at him as he was walking away, "You'll never lay eyes on this baby," and he never did.

## Not a Happy Birthday

I had a beautiful pregnancy, this fifth pregnancy. The best I ever had, but memories that had tormented me all my life would creep back. One memory was the picket gate. Every time I saw a picket gate I didn't want to live. I had to walk past a house with a picket gate on my way to work and I wondered why I felt this way.

I got a job at a factory that made oil gauges. Most of girls I worked with were German. I really got a charge out of them. The first day I was there they asked me my name. I told them my first name. They asked about my last name. I said, "Puddin' Tane." It was a goofy nursery rhyme I once heard.

Then they asked me where I lived. I said, "In a house." They asked how many children I had. The first woman who asked me, I said two. The next woman who asked me,

I said three. Next time, I said six. All these women ate their lunch together. I sat alone and ate mine.

When they got together they compared stories. They all came to me and said, "You told this woman you had two kids and this woman you had six. How many kids do you really have?"

I said, "I have a handful of nosy women and it's none of your business."

My boss was a swell guy. I ran a press. One day I went to put an oil gauge on the conveyer belt and sparks started flying off the ends of my fingers. I wasn't thinking about my own life, but my child's life. My boss laughed, "It's just a good scare. None of these presses are grounded, so all you folks go home and come back tomorrow morning. Everything will be okay."

They worked all night grounding the presses. I hung around. I said to my boss, "There's still packing to do; I'll stay and do that." He said, "Marie, go home." I said, "There's nobody at home waiting for me." He said, "Okay, you won't get paid overtime for it." I said, "I don't care."

There was a seventeen-year-old kid that I used to make fun of because he couldn't keep up with me. I had just gotten out of speed school and I couldn't work slow. I felt sorry for that kid. Me and the kid did the packing and were done in an hour and fifteen minutes. The boss came out and said, "You even swept the floor." I said, "There's nothing else for me to do."

I looked at the calendar and it was July. I thought of my

son; his birthday was the twenty-fifth. He was turning two years old. I wondered if I could save enough money and go back to Omaha for his birthday.

I went to see my boss. "Can I get a leave of absence?" I asked. He said, "No, I depend on you. I couldn't let you go. You're my best operator. I'd have to hire someone else. We've only got three more days on those parts."

I began crying, "I want to go see my kids." He said, "I don't know what to tell you."

"Can you call the airport and find out how much it would cost me to fly? I've only been in a plane once. Do you think I could leave on a Friday as soon as a I got off work then come back here on Sunday night and be to work on Monday morning?" He said, "Oh yes, you'd have plenty of time."

He called the airport and made arrangements for me. I bought a huge cake and a present. It cost me thirty-five dollars. A limousine picked me up and took me to the airport. I boarded the plane and went to Omaha.

When I got there I called my sister Faith's house. She wasn't at home. She had left her husband and was living with my brother and his wife.

When I got to my brother's house my sister-in-law wouldn't let me in. One time she and I had had a big fight and she didn't want me in her house. My brother was drunk and had locked himself in the bathroom, so he was no help to me. I ended up sleeping in their car. The front seat was full of lumps. What a night.

The next day I took the cake and birthday present and went to see my kids. The kids were gone. The woman who had been keeping the children let them go live with her husband's brother and his wife in Wabash, Indiana. They couldn't have any children of their own.

She gave me the phone number to where they were. I called the house and said, "I want my kids." They said, "You set foot on this porch and we'll call the police." Had I known then what I know today I would have called the police, walked right in there, got my kids, and walked out. They had no legal right. They had come over the state line and taken my children. I had never been informed that my children were adopted out to a couple in Indiana. I did not sign any papers to give up my kids.

I wasn't an unfit mother in any way. Many years later when I filed for divorce, the same judge that handled the divorce also handled my kids' adoption. He told me, "Mrs. Grine, you were never an unfit mother. In fact, you were very caring mother, but I do not approve of interracial marriages."

I was sick to the core of my soul. When I got back to my brother's house I straightened the front room and bed-room. Then I went to the kitchen and washed the dishes. I was taking a nap on the sofa when my sister Faith came home. We got into a big argument because I hadn't cleaned the gas stove. She got mad and yanked me off the sofa and socked me with her fist. She didn't know I was pregnant.

I went out the door and she grabbed the back of my

coat. I put my arms behind me, turning the coat sleeves wrong side out and flung it in the mud. She said, "Your beautiful coat is lying in the mud. Come back and get it." I said, "So you can beat me some more? You can keep the coat."

I don't know who ate the cake.

*Marie and I enjoyed a long friendship—over ten years. I know she let me get closer than most because I respected her. Over many experiences we had together she had earned that respect. One of those experiences was when I was called home to Alabama when my father had a heart attack.*

*It was a devastating time for me, watching my father slip away, sitting with him in the hospital. I'd come home exhausted, and more times than not, there in the mailbox would be an envelope with loopy cursive addressed to me. Just a note from Marie to remind me God loved me, that He was taking care of my dad. How did she get my address? The very idea of Marie was so foreign in this small southern town. I treasure those notes; I still have them. It amazes me that in the midst of trying to survive she took time to send me a note just so I wouldn't feel forgotten.*

—Rebecca Hill

I wanted the baby that I was carrying, but what I really wanted were the children that I had lost. I came back to Milwaukee feeling very peculiar, weak, and tired. I went to work the next morning. I didn't feel so good. The girl next to me said, "Did you eat breakfast?"

I answered, "Not much, orange juice and toast." I didn't feel right. I told the girl to open the window. "I'm having trouble breathing." She said, "There's plenty of air in here." It was about eleven o'clock. The next thing I knew I was grabbing at her shirt. I passed out colder than a cucumber. A big man carried me in and put me on the lunch table.

When I opened my eyes I said, "Why am I laying on the lunch table?" He said, "Marie, you fainted. You passed out cold." I said, "Let me off this table." He told me to lie still. There was an older woman who put a cool washcloth on my head. She said, "I don't think you should go back to work." My boss said, "We're going to send you home in a cab." I said, "But I need the money." He said, "You're in no shape to work. I want you to go home and rest and eat a big meal and take a shower and go back to bed." So I did. Everything was okay; I went back to work.

My belly was getting bigger all the time. The bigger it got the happier I was. I wore a big old sweater to cover my stomach. One day the boss was standing behind me staring right at me. I felt my skin crawl. I thought, "What in the world is he doing?" He walked up to me and said, "I want to see you in the front office."

I said, "Oh, my gosh, what have I done now?"

He said, "It's not anything that you've done. I want to ask you something and I want you to tell me the truth. Are you pregnant?"

I answered, "Yes."

Great big tears came to his eyes, "I hate to lose you, but our insurance doesn't cover pregnant women in the work place. I have to let you go."

I was stunned, "Where can I go, who's going to hire me?"

"I don't know, Marie." He gave me the money he owed me and wished me good luck. I walked out of the factory.

When I got home I counted my money; it wasn't much. There were no groceries in my cupboard, but I had paid my rent three months in advance. How was I going to eat? I needed car fare. I needed a job, but I didn't want to spend money on a newspaper. I walked down the street and asked a man, "Do you know of anyone that would have an evening paper?" He said, "Yeah, I got one." I saw a classified ad for a job on Fourth Street, within walking distance of my house.

I walked down to Fourth and discovered it was a bar. I walked in. There was a goofy-looking guy behind the bar. He had very thick glasses. I said, "Good evening." He didn't answer me. I said, "I saw this ad in the paper. I'd like to talk to the person that does the hiring." He said, "That's my father. You'll have to wait till he comes to work. He won't be here for three hours." I asked if I could wait for him at the bar. The goofy-looking guy motioned to a booth in the back. I sat and finished looking over the classifieds.

I saw another ad where they needed a sandwich maker. I thought I'd check out that place since I had the time. I was worried I might need a physical to work there. I didn't need to have a physical, and they hired me right away. I went to work that night. I loved the girls that worked with me. There was a mixture of all sorts of people—a funny atmosphere. The money was fair and the work was exciting.

Later on I went back to the first bar. I saw the most handsome man behind the counter. He was Greek with silver hair in deep waves, beautiful, and a gorgeous smile. When I walked in, he nodded and said, "Good evening. Can I help you?" I said, "I hope so. I'm looking for the father of the man that was here last evening." He said, "I'm his father." I said, "You don't look like him." He said, "He looks like his mother." "Oh," I said. "It says in the paper that you need a woman to make sandwiches and serve behind the lunch counter." He said, "We do, but I can't pay you very much. The most I can pay you is forty dollars a week. I don't think you can live on that, can you?" I said, "Not really, but I have another job and I can hold down both of them." He said, "Are you sure?" I said, "Yeah, I can for a while."

"We'll try you out."

"When?"

"Right now."

So I started then and there. I put on a hair net and a big white apron and listened while he showed me around. There were two counters in the bar, one for liquor and one for food. We had a limited menu of soup, chili, and sandwiches. I worked for a couple of hours that first day. The man behind the counter congratulated me, "Marie, you're the best waitress we ever had here. You're hired. If you have to give up one of the jobs, don't give up this one."

I loved working at the Trojan Bar. A lot of different customers came in, many of the them from the raceway nearby. But most of all I loved Charlie, the bar owner. I never met anyone who cared so much about me and how I was getting along.

One night there was a stranger in the bar who had no place to go. I didn't like his looks or his attitude and I sure wasn't looking for sex. But I felt sorry for him and took him back to my apartment. I said, "The only place to sleep is on a sofa which opens up into a bed, but I have clean sheets and pillowcases and blankets."

I went to hang up his coat and a gun dropped out. I said, "What do you call this?" He said, "Give me that." I gave it to him, "Take that gun and your coat and get out of here right now."

He went out and called the police on me. The cops came up and looked in my closet, "Where did you get this fur coat?" I said, "I bought it." The cops didn't believe me, "You got the receipt?" I said, "I don't know what I did with it." "How much did you pay for that hi-fi?" I said, "I don't remember."

"This fella claims you stole it from him."

"What? I bought all that stuff."

The cops dragged me down to the station. I begged them to call Charlie at the bar. He'd explain that I was working and earning a living. "Please call the bar." They didn't call the bar, but took me out there. I was crying like a house on fire. "Charlie, tell the policeman the truth. This man didn't have a place to go. I took him home because I felt sorry for him. Then a gun fell out of his coat and I told him to get out. He has it on him right now." They searched him and pulled out the gun. Charlie asked, "Was this your way of getting even?" He said, "Yeah, and I'm still going to get even with her."

They didn't arrest me but I ended up losing my apartment.

Charlie offered to let me store my things in the back room. I could tell Charlie was worried about me. "Marie, are you pregnant?" I lied to him, but finally broke down crying, "I've lied as long as I can. Yes, I am pregnant."

He said, "Marie, I can't have you working here." I was too scared to cry. I said, "I don't have any place to go. I lost my apartment already. What little money I did have in the bank is now gone."

He said, "Don't worry. You can stay here. I'll let you sleep in the room behind the bar."

So I stayed at the bar. I sewed baby dresses and began collecting diapers and baby shirts, baby blankets, and things I needed. I earned a little extra money at the bar by playing the piano. People gave me quarters, nickels, and dimes and told me to go play a song. I got enough clothes for the baby by doing that.

I met another man at the Trojan Bar where I worked. His name was Wally Werner. Wally spent most of his time in the bar drinking. He was a very small balding man. He had a nervous shifty-eyed demeanor. He made me feel uncomfortable around him. To top it off someone told me he had been in a mental hospital. I didn't know what the matter was with him, but I distrusted him.

One night there was no place to sleep. The bar was having a big party and I couldn't stay there that night. Charlie said, "Wally, take her home with you."

I was afraid of Wally. I said, "Come on, I don't want to go to a house of strangers where I don't know anybody."

Wally said, "My mother has a ten-room house."

I went with him and met his mother, his one brother, and two sisters. I loved his mother, Elsa. Lily, the oldest sister, drank, and the younger girl had no experience in anything. She hadn't even finished high school, no diploma. Wally was the oldest and his younger brother was Arly. They were all living off their poor daddy's wages and he didn't make very much as a janitor. I never got to know his father—he was always gone or sleeping.

Mom Elsa and I didn't agree on everything. I didn't think it was right for her grown children to live at home and not support the family. None of them were working. I told her what I thought about it. She told me that two of her oldest children had had nervous breakdowns. I said, "That is no excuse. If they are well, they should be able to hold down some sort of job to help. Deliver papers or something."

### Rebecca

When I was eight months pregnant, I got a real sharp pain in my stomach. Always before I felt a quivering and then went into labor. So I thought, "I can't be in labor, maybe this is a forewarning." I sat down and another wave of sharp pains came over me. I waited and there was no more pain, so I forgot about it. I was living over the bar at this time and was preparing to go downstairs. I reached for the handrail when another pain shot through me; I grabbed my belly and hollered. Charlie ran up to me and helped me get downstairs. He insisted that I go to the hospital to get it checked out.

I took a streetcar out to the hospital. The doctor said, "Lady, you're about to have this baby.

They examined me and found that I had a fistula. A while ago I had had a boil, but the doctor hadn't taken out the core. From sitting on the hard stools of the factory and at the bar, the core had gone higher inside of me forming a fistula. The skin around my rectum was very soft. I don't know if these doctors used this for an excuse, but they wanted me to have a cesarean. The student doctor said, "Marie, we're afraid to have a natural birth. The skin is too soft. The baby might come through the wrong channel and burst the skin. I want you to sign for a C-section." I signed.

I didn't trust doctors. When I got to the operating room I learned that I was the subject of a medical class. The room was full of medical students all staring at me and pointing to my stomach. There was a huge light so bright you couldn't look at it. These students sat way up high all around me. A doctor came and said, "I'm going to be your doctor. I will bring your baby into the world."

They put a steel thing on my jaw and strapped me down below the knees and under my armpits. They injected needles into my arms. The nurse gave me ether and that's all I remembered.

When I came to, I said, "God, let me die." It felt like a hot iron was on my belly. Wally came to see me, but I couldn't see his face. He left and went back to the bar and told them I was dying. Charlie got upset. Every time I came to I could hear a machine doing my breathing for me. It scared me. Then they put me in the main room where no one slept because I moaned all the time.

I didn't see my baby until five days later. They had to keep me knocked out. The first time I saw my baby I wept. I had a beautiful, healthy girl. She was pretty, but had no hair, just peach fuzz. I named her after Charlie. Her full name was Glenda Rebecca Charlee. When Charlie found out he acted angry, but I think he liked that I named the baby for him. He came over and put his hand on my shoulder and squeezed it.

I gave her Wally's last name. In the hospital they said, "Who's this guy?" I said, "He's my husband." I was afraid if they knew I wasn't married they would take my baby out to the Catholic home. Wally didn't care.

When I was released I called the bar, "Is Charlie there?" They said, "He's busy." I asked where Wally was. They told me he was busy drinking. I tried to explain, "This is Marie. I'm at the hospital and was released an hour ago. I want to come back to the bar."

I had enough money to take the streetcar, but it was so cold. It was February 1951. I wasn't afraid for myself, but I was afraid my baby might catch a chill. Wally came out and got me. I told him to bring some clean clothes for the baby. I had two little bread sacks. One had dirty clothes in it and the other one had the baby's new clothes. He brought the dirty clothes because he had been drinking. The nurse told me not to cry.

We got to the bar and got out of the cab. Wally paid the cab. He said, "Let's go in the bar." I said, "No, I don't need that bar anymore. I've got what I want. I don't think a bar is any place to take a child. I don't want my baby christened by a bar, but by the church."

He looked at me real funny and looked down at the ground. He looked like he was crying. He said, "Marie, if you don't go into that bar there's going to be a lot of people hurt."

"What are you talking about? No one cares about me, except Charlie." Suddenly I saw old Charlie—he had climbed up on the ledge outside the first floor window. He hollered and motioned for me to come inside.

I said, "No, Charlie, I don't want to go in there." He begged me to come in.

Finally, I gave in. "Okay, just to say hello.'" Wally flung the door open big and wide and pushed me in. I almost dropped my baby. There was over one hundred people waiting for me. All the tables and chairs were pulled back.

At the hospital I thought nobody cared. "What are all those boxes against the wall stacked to the ceiling?" I asked.

"Marie, that's for you."

"What? You're kidding." They handed me a mayonnaise jar with a slit in the top. It was stuffed full of money, two hundred dollars. They said, "Even Max put in a twenty-dollar bill." And Max was a Jew.

Charlie cried and laughed. The look of surprise on my face thrilled him. He laughed until the tears were just rolling.

Frank turned around on his stool, looking at me and the baby. He had a peculiar expression on his face. I asked, "Frank, what's the matter? Is something wrong?" He said, "I was just looking around the bar. Your baby doesn't have any hair does it?" I said, "No, just some peach fuzz."

He said, "As I'm looking around the bar the only bald one in here is Max. It must be Max's baby." I burst out laughing and everyone in the room just roared. Max would always walk back and forth looking for money on the ground. There was a dime lying right on the counter. He was so excited about me and the baby he didn't even see the dime. They said, "Max, you're slipping."

Some gay people came regularly to the bar. At first I had resented them. I didn't let them know it but I was ashamed to be seen with them because of the way I was raised. Well that night they gave me eight boxes all full of things for the baby. One gave me her wedding dress. It was beautiful chiffon with gobs and gobs of lace. She said, "Marie, I'll never use it and my daughters don't want it. I see you sitting and sewing a lot. Could you make some baby dresses out of this?" I said, "I sure could. One of the first things I'm going to do is make myself a petticoat." I cried so hard that night when I thought of all the ill feelings I had held toward the gays.

### Charlie

Later somebody rented an apartment for me, paid three months' rent. I never did find out who, but I think Charlie did it. It was a special time for me to be alone with Rebecca. I didn't want anyone around. I was in heaven; she was a good baby. I nursed her and dressed her in beautiful clothes and took her with me everywhere. I sure was happy.

I had to make a payment on my washing machine so I asked one of the gays to babysit Rebecca. On the way to the appliance store I had to walk past the Trojan Bar. It was a warm day and I stopped in to get a squirt of soda pop.

Charlie said, "Marie, I've got a problem. You see this bag here?" I nodded my head. The bag had the words "First National Bank" printed in big black letters on it. "What's the matter, Charlie?"

"This bag has to get to the bank and I can't close the bar."

I asked about his son or daughter, but they were both busy. "What about your wife?" "My wife is a society woman and has gone to a bridge club. I want you to take this to the bank and just hand it to the cashier. Walk straight down there, don't talk to anybody, just smile. When you go in the bank, just say good morning and give it to the bank teller. Say it's from Charlie at the Trojan bar."

I said, "Okay." The bank was only about six blocks from the bar.

I walked in and did exactly as Charlie said. I walked out of the bank and then walked to the store to pay for my washing machine.

Later, I stopped in to see Charlie. "I took the bag to the bank," I said.

"Marie, do you know how much money was in that sack?"

I was stunned, "What? Cash?"

"Yeah. There was over ten thousand dollars in cash."

If I had known what was in the bag I would have never taken it. I would have been scared to death. "Charlie, how did you know you could trust me?"

He said, "Marie, I know you."

One time I had to leave Rebecca with Charlie. I said, "Charlie, I don't know what to do. I have to go see Wally's mother about something. The window of his car is out and I'm afraid to take the baby because it is quite a drive. I'm afraid she'll get a chill. I don't know what in the world to do. I can't find a babysitter. Do you know of anyone?"

He said, "Yeah, I know somebody."

I asked who.

He said, "Me."

"Charlie, you can't take care of that baby. You're a man; you don't know how to take care of a baby." He told me he had helped out quite a bit raising his son and daughter because his wife was so busy.

Finally, I relented. I asked Wally to drive me out to his mom's as quick as he could and then get me back because I was worried about my baby. I was worried that someone might go off their nut and start throwing bottles.

So I took care of my business with Wally's mother. But oh, did it get cold in that car. Good thing I didn't take the baby. When I got back Rebecca was sound asleep up on some beer cases and her pants were as dry as a bone.

I said, "Well, Charlie, you are the first man I've ever known to take such good care of a baby. I would never be afraid to leave my baby with you." He had fixed a spot for Rebecca that would be safe even if someone did start throwing beer bottles.

Charlie sure was a wonderful person.

But Wally was a different kind of person. He was one of

those I had extreme difficulty understanding. He didn't do kind things very often. I do remember one time when he was really considerate. We were driving out with the baby to see his mother. How Wally ever got a driver's license I'll never know. He had repaired the window in his old car so that the wind couldn't come in, but all of a sudden it blew out. I unbuttoned my coat and put the baby inside my coat as quick as I could because she only had on a baby bunting. Cold air was rushing in and I shouted at Wally to stop. He braked right in the middle of the road. It's a miracle we didn't get hit. He took off his overcoat and wrapped it around the baby. That was probably the kindest thing he ever did for me.

Later I was to regret that I ever laid eyes on Wally.

### *Margaret*

Wally and I were never boyfriend and girlfriend, but I did have sex with him. I didn't want to. The reason I did was because of his mother. I loved his mother; she was a wonderful, wonderful person. I thought if I could have a child for Wally's mother that would make her happy. Also I wanted to repay the debt that I owed these people.

Wally loved Rebecca, my baby by Gail, but Margaret was his own child. Rebecca was one year old when Margaret was born in 1952. I was twenty-six years old.

Shortly before she was born, I had the most peculiar thing happen to me. While I was waiting for the doctors to wheel me downstairs for another cesarean, I said, "Doc, can you take a look at this." My stomach involuntarily peaked like a mountain and then would flatten out. "What in the world is going on?" The doctor laughed and explained that the baby was up on its knees. I believed then that my baby was a token from God. She was up on her knees praying.

After the baby was bathed I asked to see her. The nurse told me, "Your baby has been put in the state's care." I was dumbfounded. The doctors and nurses wouldn't let me get out of bed. Finally, Wally's mother came to see me. I was crying my heart out. I grabbed Mom.

"What in the world is the matter, Marie?"

"My baby is gone; they've taken her to the orphanage."

Mom didn't believe me. The orphanage was right across the street and down one block. Mom said, "Marie, watch out, get out of my road." She went out to the nurses station shouting at the top of her voice. "I'll just give you twenty minutes to get my grandchild back up here. My husband works for the city. I will have this place sued for everything it's got. This baby is my granddaughter and you don't treat any relative of mine like that." They almost killed themselves getting that baby back in the nursery.

I held baby Margaret; ruddy and red she was. Her face was one long nose and, oh, she was as skinny as a crow. She was an ugly baby, but she turned out to be a very beautiful girl.

She looked like a skinny little sparrow lying there. Mom asked me what I had named her and I said, "I named her

for you." Wally's mother's name was Elsa Lorraine Werner.
I tried Lorraine and that didn't sound right so I named her
Elsa Margaret Werner, but we called her Margaret.

I had to leave both children at Mom's place because I
had to stay at the hospital for more surgery. I was in the
hospital about five weeks without seeing my Margaret. I
was furious with my doctor. I said, "Doc, I've been here
almost five weeks. If you don't release me I'm going to walk
out to the front desk and sign myself out. I've had a belly
full of this."

He told me I could sign myself out if I wanted to, but I
couldn't come back if I got an infection. "We don't have to
take you back."

"Oh, that's how it is."

He said, "That's right. You can take the chance if you
want to."

"Okay, doc, you win, you win."

I thought I was going nuts from boredom and wanting
to go home. I went out to the sunporch and looked at the
magazines. I knew those magazines by heart. Outside little squirrels were playing in the leaves and the sun was
going down. It was a beautiful, beautiful evening.

I was sitting in this room feeling very, very lonely without my babies when a woman came bursting in through the
swinging doors of the hospital corridor. She was carrying a
bundle and her face was as white as death. I got up to see
what was happening.

A blanket fell off and I saw the blue face of a baby, like

a lifeless doll. She looked at me and asked for a doctor. I pointed to the nurses station. I thought for sure the woman was going to drop the baby before she got up to the nurses desk. She handed her baby to a doctor; he said about six words and closed the door.

The mother was almost in hysterics. I sat there and watched her for a little bit and then I went over and put my arm around her. She told me to get away from her. I said, "I'll remove my arm, but I'm not going to get away from you because at a time like this it is not too good for you to be alone; you need somebody."

"How would you know?"

I waited and then said, "I just know." She was crying something terrible; snot was running out her nose and hanging way down. I happened to have a brand new packet of Kleenex in my pocket so I took three or four of them out and handed them to her. She thanked me.

I said, "Maybe you don't need a lot of talking, but I've got broad shoulders. If you feel like talking I'll listen to anything you have to say." I paused a moment, "I just want to ask you one thing—do you believe there is a God?"

She looked at me really funny. "I don't know. I don't know if there is or not." She told me the story of what had happened. She was busy fixing supper; her husband was on his way home from work. She had two small children. She had formula on the countertop in a jar for the baby. She had forgotten that earlier that day she had mixed up boric acid in a jar to set out for some roaches. She had a problem with roaches. Instead of giving the baby the formula she accidentally gave the baby a bottle with the boric acid solution. She was afraid it was fatal.

"Do you know how to pray?" She shook her head no. I said, "I'll tell you what I'm going to do. I'm going to bow my head and pray right now."

I can't remember what I said. I remembered the pain I felt when I lost my son Douglas—all the sorrow—and I was amazed by God's timing that He would allow me to bring comfort to this woman. I asked that Jesus would show this woman mercy.

Much later the doctor came back out of the swinging doors. The woman jumped to her feet but didn't rush over to him. She was afraid of what he was going to say. She looked up at the doctor with a horrible expression on her face, half hope and half fear. She asked, "Is he, is he . . ." She was afraid to say the word "dead."

The doctor said, "I'll tell you what, let's look." He had a nurse bring out the baby. The baby was completely covered. He took the cover off the baby's face and the child was grinning from ear to ear and waving his hands. The mother had a look of disbelief; she couldn't believe what she was seeing.

Then he took the blanket off the baby's feet and they were kicking good and strong. As soon as she saw the baby's feet kicking, she snatched—not reached, but snatched—the baby out of the doctor's arms. She didn't say thank you or anything. The cover was half off her baby and she tried to cover him while walking away.

As she got to the swinging doors she stopped, pivoted on one foot, and came back as if she forgot something. She walked up to me and took one of my hands. I'll never forget what she said. She said, "Lady, I don't know who you are and I'll probably never ever see you again, but as long as you live you will never know what you did for me."

I said, "Well, honey, all I did was talk to you."

She said, "Oh, no, you gave me hope when there was none. I just want to say thanks." She waved her arm to the doctor to thank him and walked out the door. I never did see her again.

After she left my cheeks itched a little bit. I discovered that my face was wet from tears. I had been crying and didn't know it. My tears were tears of joy. I thought to myself, "How can this be, this can't be real."

It was the strangest sensation to think I might possibly have been used by God. At that moment, I was not in this world, I was in a world that was created for me. Once again I was holding my little boy on my lap. I had him on my knee; I had a hold of his two little hands and I was jigging him up and down. He was throwing his head back laughing, and I was so happy.

I looked up at a calendar on the wall in the nurses station. I couldn't believe it—it was five years to the very day that my little boy had passed away.

I just wish there was some way I could pass on hope to people who have lost loved ones. Great blessings are waiting in store for them because of the suffering. I believe this is something that God Himself has fixed for people so that they can be comforted and given hope when there is none. God will point to another door which has opened in their life.

### Cal and the Chesterfield

When I went to get Margaret back, Mom and the Werners wouldn't let me have her. I was still in a daze from surgery. I knew I had had a baby and wanted her desperately. I moved with Rebecca back to the Trojan and lived up above the bar. Later I moved to Fourth Street and Juneau.

One of the girls I met on Fourth and Juneau when Rebecca was quite small was Sally Patterson. I liked her even though she was full-blooded German. She was a tall girl about six foot one and had been hurt a lot, and deep. Sally understood me and I understood her. We were very close friends for many years.

During the brief time I lived with Sally, Rebecca and I were very happy. There was a beautiful feeling inside of me, almost a power to think I might be a comfort to people who were hurting. That time in the hospital helped me to realize this. For the first time in my life I felt like I was of value, valuable to other people, valuable to God, a richness in the center of my soul.

Soon all the bad premonitions I had about Wally came to a head. He called the cops on me and made me lose my two girls. I'll never ever forgive him for that. The state took my kids in 1953. Rebecca was about two, Margaret about one. All my children were gone. My life has repeated itself so many times and in so many sad ways.

I really hit the skids. I thought about suicide all the time. I didn't care about anything. I couldn't work, wouldn't take a bath, I stopped combing my hair. I slept on the ground. I lost many, many years living like this.

I found another bar east of the Trojan, closer to the river, closer to the lake. It was called the Chesterfield. There was an old man behind that bar, too. He liked me, but I didn't have a close relationship with him like I had had with Charlie. He protected me. He knew I didn't want the men to pat me or anything. He'd yell at the men, "Hey, hey, you. Don't do that in here."

I made money while I was in the Chesterfield. I learned how to hit the pinball machines. Men in the bar would place bets on the machines. I figured out how to push the buttons and how to get the numbers. I earned some money while making a fool out of myself.

I took that money and I rented a place. I didn't care how I looked. I didn't even wash my face unless I got so miserable I couldn't stand it anymore.

I started dating a man. I met him at the bar. His name was Pete Columbo Pierre Augustini. What a name. Everyone called him Cal. He was full-blooded Italian.

We were sitting at the bar and I had taken a metal initial and fixed it on my purse. It was the initial *M*. He said to me, "What does that stand for?" I told him, "It stands for me, my name, Marie." We started talking and became friends.

Cal had an apartment not too far from the bar. I told Cal, "I can't be sitting at this bar three or four hours before you get off work." At the Trojan I was a drawing card. The men used to come in there just to talk with me. They found me exciting to talk to, but at the Chesterfield I couldn't hang out like that.

Cal said, "I'll tell you what I'll do, Marie. I'll give you the key to my apartment. You just go up there and wait for me. Don't think you're walking into something fancy, it just has a refrigerator, a bed, and a gas stove."

I went up to his apartment. It was winter time, and I took off my coat, hat, and scarf. I sat in an arm chair for awhile and then got up to make some coffee. In the cupboard I couldn't find any coffee, so I poured myself a glass of milk. I thought about fixing a sandwich and opened a tray in the refrigerator where I thought the lunchmeat would be stored. Inside the hydrator was a great big chunk of bloody ice. I stood there staring at it just like I was transfixed. My hands were hanging onto the pan and I thought for sure I was going to pass out. I looked up above and saw that some hamburger meat had thawed and dripped blood down into the tray.

Boy oh boy, I did plenty of thinking. I didn't even make the sandwich, I lost complete interest, but I did drink the milk. When Cal came in I told him that something terrible had happened to me. He was very concerned and he asked what had happened. I told him about the bloody ice in the tray. He didn't get it; he started laughing. I said, "You can laugh if you want to, but I want to mark this day on a calendar."

### Painful Memories

I went to see Rebecca and Margaret. They were living just a short distance from Mitchell Street—which is on the south side of Milwaukee. I started making regular visits to see them. Not too long after that I got a job though I began having fainting spells and pain in my chest. I didn't tell anyone about these problems.

Cal and I were living together in an apartment and I had got myself a darling little dog. We did a considerable amount of traveling and always took the dog with us. We sure had a lot of fun with that little dog.

On one of our travels we paid a visit to Cal's mother's place in Michigan. His mother and father were very nice to me, but I sensed there was something wrong in the home. I couldn't put my finger on it.

Coming back to Milwaukee we started going over a bridge. It was at least two hundred feet straight down. Cal said, "I have a notion to take this car and run it right through the bridge." Now the bridge abutment was only about two feet high concrete on both sides. I said, "Cal, if you are determined to do something like that, my God, let me and my little dog out." Then it seemed like his mind sort of cleared and we went on home.

Another night we were coming home from the supermarket. There was an old man crossing the street. We were in the car and Cal said, "I have a good notion to kill that sucker. Just run this car into him and kill him." I said, "Cal, what makes you say a thing like that?"

I was really happy when my little dog had puppies. Then one night when I came home from work a puppy was dead. I took the poor little thing down by the lake and buried it. After that every night there would be another puppy dead, Finally, there were no puppies. I felt the mother; she had plenty of milk. I couldn't comprehend what was going on.

Though Cal and I slept side by side, there was no sex between us. He was always complaining about his back. Sometimes he would put his hand on his back and his face looked just like a dead man. I told him to go to a doctor. He was afraid he would lose his job. The pain got so bad, he started saying crazy things to me just like my foster mother used to. My foster mother always made feel inferior like I wasn't like other people. Cal started doing that.

For instance, one thing that really got on his nerves was some fuzz underneath the radiator. He said, "My God, Marie, why don't you ever dust and mop these floors?"

"Well, Cal, I'm holding down a job, I'm taking care of this dog, I'm running this apartment, I'm cooking meals, I'm going shopping, I'm trying to help you as much as I can. I'm tired that's all."

He said, "My sister kept a house neater than this." I let that upset me which was very very foolish of me. I was doing more than most of the women in my block. Considering all that I had been through I thought I was doing okay. Then one day there was rip in my dress. It was a rip behind my arm. He yelled at me. It was just little things like that, you know.

Also, I was having trouble on my job. Some of the other women and I got into it with the foreman. They finally fired me. I was lucky; I had our rent paid up two or three months in advance, so I stayed home for a couple weeks.

The pain in Cal's back grew to be unbearable. He finally did ask for a leave of absence at his job and went straight to the hospital. He was only in the hospital twenty minutes when they diagnosed his case. He had a tumor on his spine as big as a golf ball. The specialists said he should have been dead or else insane, one of the two. The tumor was pressing on the nerves that went to his heart and brain.

The doctors at the hospital told Cal to sign a release statement saying he was aware he might die on the operating table. "We cannot promise anything because it is in a very touchy spot. Other nerves travel through there, a conjunction of connecting nerves. You might end up a cripple for life." Cal said, "I don't care, I'll sign the papers. I want to be operated on immediately."

I cracked up. Things just were too much for me, between trouble at work, trouble with Cal, the dead puppies, and the bloody ice. I couldn't figure out why all these things were happening. I told the lady upstairs that I was going to check into the Milwaukee County Hospital because I had mental problems which I could not solve. I wasn't crazy, but I needed help.

I went out to the mental clinic. I hesitated before I signed myself in. I prayed. It was the mistake of my life. I didn't get any help at all. The psychiatrist kept asking me, "Do you have bad dreams, flashbacks." I said, "Yes." He said, "I can't see anything wrong with you. Why in the world are you in this hospital?"

I answered because I was tearing up my clothes trying to get at that feeling inside of me. "That's not normal," I said. "I have a feeling inside of me that I can't explain, a sick feeling. I don't know what to do about it. I can't stand it."

I signed in, hoping I would get help. After being locked in there for three weeks with mental patients and no place to go, you really do get goofy. I was released within three weeks. They said they couldn't find anything wrong with me. They sent me right back to the same hole I climbed out of. I went back to the same apartment where I cracked up. You can't do that. You have to make a break, a brand new start. My little dog was gone. I was really upset about that. I went out to the hospital to see Cal. I cracked up again at the hospital.

*It was late November of 1987. It had been three weeks since my wife left me. The pain of rejection, the fear of what was going to happen were like the coming of winter. Inescapable.*

*"Hi, Jon," said a familiar guttural voice. I turned; Marie looked into my face and asked the one question I absolutely did not feel like answering. "How's the wife and kids?"*

*Her breath streamed out into the evening air, now lit by streetlamps. I took, exhaled a breath of my own. And I told her how things were. Her puffy, roughened hand brushed back a stray strand of gray hair. "How can that be?" she asked herself. "How can that be?"*

*I had no response to her twice-asked question. But I was vulnerable to her caring: who was the street person, who was the Jesus person?*

*"I had my breakdown and they took my kids away. In the mental institution I felt nothing but despair. Then one day, when I had decided to end it all, I looked out my window. It was just after a storm. The trees were changed, diamond-coated with ice. God said to me, 'Marie, I can transform your life just like I transformed these trees.' And God can do that for you too, Jon!"*

*I stared at this plain woman, stunned. And I am stunned still by the wonder of it. Marie's story had been given to me as an offering, a balm of easement for my pain. Marie's tears, shed during the telling of her story to me, were the tears of Jesus Christ Himself.*

—Jon Trott

## Barren Trees

So I went back to the mental hospital for the second time. They admitted me. A man came out and called my name, "Marie." He said, "I'm sorry, I must have the wrong one." I asked, "Is there another Marie here?" He said, "Yeah, the Marie I'm calling is on her way to the state mental hospital."

I said, "You've got to be joking. Are you sure you have the right person?" He said he was sure. He said they were going to take me tomorrow morning to the state hospital for the mentally insane. I said, "Man, I'm not insane."

The doctor walked out. I got up from the chair real slow, walked to the door that was locked and leaned against it. I cried like my heart was broken. I heard two nurses yell, "Watch that woman!" They thought I was going to go berserk. I couldn't believe what was happening to me. It was worse than being in a daze.

The next morning the aids came and asked if I was ready to go. I said I was ready. It was Thanksgiving Day, 1960.

Riding along, I said to myself, "This is the end. This is all she wrote for me. I'll go to that hospital and I'll never get out."

I closed my eyes and didn't talk to anybody the whole time I was riding. There was a woman sitting in front of us and there was another woman sitting between me and a lady going to the women's prison.

I looked out the window. I couldn't cry. If I could have cried it would have been so much easier, but I couldn't shed a tear. I prayed, prayed harder than I've ever prayed in my life. I said, "God if your hand is in this thing please prove it to me. I've got to have some comfort."

I stared out the window as the empty dirt fields passed by. There had been a terrible, terrible wind storm. In the middle of a field was a tree, its branches spread out every which way. The tree was stripped of leaves, barren, black, and ugly. I saw one branch, broken loose and hanging by a splinter.

I thought, "Why doesn't somebody cut that off and haul it away?" God spoke to my heart. He said, "Marie, your life is not over. Do you see that black branch? This is your stay in the state hospital. That tree is going to go on living and so will you. You are going to have a beautiful life."

I said, "God, it is so hard to believe that right now, but it must be true. Why else would you have shown me this?" I rode along not talking with anyone, but feeling a tremendous comfort inside of me.

My suffering at the Winnebago State Mental Hospital was beyond words. I call the mental hospital the devil's playground.

Entry took place right after my arrival at Kempster Hall. The attendants checked me for head and body lice. Disinfectant was poured over me; it was a wonder I had any skin left. They took away what I was wearing and issued me new clothes. When I came out on the other side I stood naked before a group of women. I thought I'd die.

Everything had a harsh echo to it, hollow, because of the steel stairwells and concrete brick walls. Every place you looked there were mental patients. There was no place to hide. If you went in the dayroom, they were in there. If you went to your own room, your roommate was there. The locker room, the dining hall, the bathroom, there was no place to go.

If I did it once, I did it a million times: I used to watch the sun go down while lying on my bed. This was my favorite time of the day. The sun was a fire red turning the snow-covered ground pink and orange. Little squirrels hopped and jumped in and out between the bare trees trying to find something to eat.

I was not mentally ill at the time I went into the clinic; I merely had a problem, but they said I had to sign myself in or I would get no help at all. After being in the clinic— I was in there twice within a period of four weeks—then I really did become mentally ill.

The reason I'm telling this is because there are terrible, terrible things that go on inside mental hospitals. My heart is bursting. There will be many times, or at least one time in almost everybody's life, when things go bad. For people who do not have a foundation, who do not feel secure, it can shake you. It can break you. That's what happened to me. I should never have been locked up.

I saw three women come in who did not appear to be mentally ill at the time, but after three weeks they acted very crazy. None of the three ever recovered, at least while I was there. I began to think I might not ever get well.

One afternoon, as usual, I was lying on my bed. I said, "Where is God in this place? Where are you, God? Where are you?" I was crying my heart out. I said, "God, if you're with me, prove it to me."

### Flowers Still Bloom

I saw a sign from God at the state mental hospital. I was very miserable that day. I was so miserable I just wanted to die. I thought to myself, "If I can't get well, if I can't get out of here, then, please, just let me die here in my bed. Let me die. Let me die!"

A woman came to my room and said, "Marie, it's time to go for lunch." I said, "I don't want to eat. I don't care if I ever eat."

"Oh, Marie, you're just in one of your moods."

"Well, maybe I am, but I can't see any sense to being locked up, and for what? I didn't do anything!"

I went with her anyway. It was twenty-three degrees below zero. That's what the guards told us anyhow. There wasn't too much snow, only about a foot and a half. The sun was shining so bright it burned my eyes. I had to use my hand to shield my eyes when I stepped outdoors.

We had gone perhaps twenty, thirty feet when I saw a flower sticking up out of the snow, right along the edge of the shoveled sidewalk. Blooming through the snow bank was a great big fat dandelion; the blossom was about as big as a fifty-cent piece. It was freezing cold outside. I cannot understand how a flower could bloom through the snow and cold, but it did; it survived. At least that's how it appeared to me.

I raised my eyes to Him and said, "God, that's all I need. That's all the proof I need to know that you are with me. When you are with me I feel like a bull, I can do anything."

That made me very bold. It gave me a lot of self-confidence. I started laughing. Some of the girls said, "Gee, Marie, you sure have changeable moods." I called the girls over to look. "Oh, please come see the flower blooming through the snow," but none of them came. They were all too sick mentally to even notice such a thing.

### Crystal Trees

I had only asked for one sign, but He gave me another because I needed it. I was receiving therapy, but I wasn't getting any better. I decided I'd deal with it as best I could. And you know, I knew if I couldn't cope, I could do away with myself. There was always that. I'd already tried it a few times. But I'd never been in so much blackness as this.

The doctors didn't find much to encourage me with. After the treatments, I'd go out into a lobby area for patients. There was a big plate-glass window looking out into the yard behind the building. The first day I was there, I saw the trees out there, gray and stripped of leaves. And those trees were me. Dead, ugly, and useless. Months passed, and one day, after another treatment, I finally decided to end it all.

I told God I was sorry but I couldn't help it. Everything was black; even the weather was miserable. Freezing rain and gloomy overcast skies. I wanted to be alone. No one was in the lobby.

Something in the room was glowing. The storm was over and the sun was out. The trees, those gray, ugly trees, were transformed. They were covered with ice crystal, every last trunk and branch and twig. The sun through those branches and twigs made them shine like a million prisms. The breeze touched the trees, and shimmering, shaking shards of light, moving, shifting and changing, rainbows and sparkling diamonds, flew everywhere. Even on me!

It was so beautiful. As I looked at those trees, I knew I was looking at myself. I heard God whisper to me, "Marie, you think you are one of those dead, barren trees, but to me you're dressed in crystal and diamonds and light."

Then I knew I could make it.

I just love that part in the Bible where it says, "I will never leave you nor forsake you." That's how I felt that cold winter day.

### Blackie

I made some beautiful friends in the state mental hospital. Closer friends than I've had in my entire life, because these people were with me twenty-four hours around the clock. I got to know them very, very well.

A lot of peculiar things happened while I was there, a lot of funny things, a lot of sad things happened. One thing that really did shock me was this. There are a lot of people inside institutions like this that have no business being there, never should have been sent there.

I got the shock of my life at how the place was run and the pull some people had. There was one girl brought in. She looked to be about twenty-four or twenty-six years old. She could have been attractive had she been fixed up, but she wasn't.

They turned her loose in Kempster Hall after she had been disinfected. Walking around real nervous and real fast, she said, "I'll be out tomorrow morning." All of us girls said, "Yeah, yeah, just like us." She said, "No, I will be. I'm somebody important's niece, I'll be out tomorrow morning." We all laughed, "Yeah, and I'm the president's wife. Who are you?"

Well, I'll be doggone; at ten o'clock the next morning a great big black limousine pulled up into the front driveway.

Sure enough, within fifteen minutes she climbed into that black limousine and rode away. I didn't know how things like that happened, but they did.

One friend I made, he wasn't so wonderful, but I was glad to have him for a friend. His name was Blackie. I used to sit with Blackie and talk. Sometimes we would just walk around on the grounds. There was a commissary you could go to, but you had to have money. We'd sit there and have a soda pop or a malt.

Most of the time I was saving my money. Every time someone gave me a nickel or a dime I'd salt it.

I got paid six cents an hour to work in the paring room. I was used to making four hundred dollars a week. I was insulted beyond words. That started the wheels turning inside my head for me to run away.

Sometimes frustration and rejection are to our own good. It is strange how God works in very peculiar ways to bring about wonderful and good things. During my stay in the mental hospital I clung to my hope in God, but even then the undercurrent was so strong; my faith hung like a silken thread. If ever someone cut that thread I would be lost forever.

### Liberty

One day I forgot to take my medicine. They took away my liberty and kept me in the ward. I was sitting in a rocking chair when suddenly I stood up and started ripping my clothes off. A nurse came in and asked what the matter was. I said, "I can't stand being locked up in here anymore." She asked, "Why are you locked up in here when everyone else is out on liberty?"

"I forgot to take my medicine one day. I was at the ball game and forgot. I came back to the main building to take my medicine, but they took my liberty away from me."

She went straight to the head doctor. She didn't waste any time. I had my release papers just like that.

If a patient ran away and was caught, they were restricted to their room. If a patient resisted and continued to try to get away, they were shackled and confined to their bed. I often thought about running away, but was afraid of being caught.

One afternoon I didn't go out on liberty right away. I sat on the side of my bed instead. The girls said, "Come on, come on, Marie, it's liberty time." I just wanted to sit on my bed and think.

While sitting there I heard my foster father speaking; he said, "Marie, why don't you use your head?" I said to myself, "That's the answer, I've got to use my head. I've got to get out of here. I've got a head, two hands, and two feet." I looked at my hands and feet and began laughing like a hyena. "Ha, ha, ha." The girls looked at me like I was cuckoo. I got right up and walked outside. I found Blackie and told him I was leaving.

Blackie tried to scare me out of running away. He knew I was gullible and would believe him. It was a beautiful summer day and we decided to take a walk around the grounds. He asked me if I ever smelled anything funny.

"Why, yes, when I first came I noticed a peculiar odor. I asked the nurses about it, but they didn't say anything."

Blackie asked me, "What would happen to you if you died? Would your family come and claim your body?"

I answered truthfully, "It is because of my foster parents that I'm in here. If they didn't want or love me when I was with them I know for certain they don't want me when I'm dead."

Blackie pointed to the smokestacks at the hospital power plant. "That's where they burn the bodies."

"What are you talking about?"

"Bodies from the state mental hospital. If nobody claims them, then they are cremated. This is a crematorium for the whole state. About five or six hundred bodies a day come through here."

I was absolutely sick. I had been eating a raw apple and had to stop eating it. I threw the whole thing away.

"You've got to be kidding." When he told me those dead bodies were being burned in there I opened my mouth to scream and before you could say Ray Robinson, Blackie had his hand over my mouth so tight it was hurting me. He dragged me off behind some bushes. I thought for sure Blackie was going to rape me.

He laid me on my back and sat right on my belly and put both hands over my mouth because I kept moving my head trying to get his hands off of me. He had me pinned down to the ground, his knees holding both wrists.

He said, "Marie, I know you are going to start screaming. I'm not going to take my hand off your mouth until
you relax and stop trying to get away from me. If they hear
you screaming you will go into a room and you will never,
never get out."

I couldn't talk because he had his hand over my mouth,
but I relaxed. I heard a bell ring. He moved his hand and I
started to scream. He quickly re-covered my mouth. "Now,
Marie, you're going to have to listen to me, because when
that second bell rings and you're not in the building, then
you really will get locked up for sure."

I relaxed and Blackie let me up, taking hold of my hand.
Blackie apologized, "I didn't want to do that but I had to
do it to keep you from being put back into the dark room."

I told Blackie I couldn't stay knowing that bodies were
being burned. I couldn't stand the thought of a crematorium on the grounds. I began planning an escape.

"Marie, you really are crazy now. Do you know what
they do to you if you get caught? They're going to put you
in chains for six weeks. They're going to chain you to a bed
on your back. You won't even be allowed to get up and use
the toilet. And when they feed you with a spoon they ram
it clear down your throat."

I said, "Well, that's the chance I got to take."

Years later I found out all of that talk about a crematorium Blackie had scared me with was a lie. It really was just
an incinerator for the institution.

## I Escape

Just a few days before I found out about the crematorium, I saw a hawk come down. The bird had swooped down for a piece of bread and, midflight, was shot down. I said to myself, "Well, if the hawk can't get in and get out, then how in the world am I going to make it out of here?"

I stopped taking my medication. I stuck it in the side of my cheek and spit it out in the toilet. I found a plastic bag and hid it under a big rock out in the cornfield. Every day I'd go to the cornfield and hide things. Underpants, bras, half-slips, blouses, Levis, anything I could get my hands on, but no food.

In the library I studied the maps. The closest city to Oshkosh was Milwaukee, but I didn't want to go back there because of the memories. I decided to go to Minneapolis, Minnesota.

Blackie said, "Marie, I can help you. I can get you past the aid's station. If I'm with you they'll think I'm your boyfriend and just let us walk past."

It was August and awfully hot. It took me about three weeks to put the whole thing together. Me and Blackie would practice each afternoon by walking together to the cornfield where my bag was hidden. I'd put some new thing in the bag and we'd walk back. I timed exactly when the aides came to work and when there was a shift change.

The day I decided to escape, I couldn't find Blackie anywhere. I checked the TV room—a man was sitting in there. He whispered to me, "Marie, I know you are leaving.

Here, I've been saving these for you. You take this packet of Lucky Strikes. Every time you get scared rub those Lucky Strikes." I thanked him and went on.

I finally found Blackie. We began to walk to the field. Blackie told me to slow down. We got to the big rock and Blackie helped me move it. He offered to carry the plastic bag to the end of the cornfield. I was crying my heart out. "Blackie, I'm so scared, please come with me." I begged him, "I can't do it alone."

"Marie, you told me you've hitchhiked all your life."

I said, "Yeah, but that's not what I'm afraid of. I'm afraid of my own emotions. I've been locked up. What if I crack up out there?"

"Whatever you do, don't turn around and look back. There is no hope for you then." Blackie and I were standing at the edge of the cornfield. He said, "Marie, this is far as I can go. You have to do the rest of it alone."

I was still crying, but no tears came. I threw my arms around his neck. Blackie raised his arm and slapped me in the face twice real hard. "Marie, wake up, wake up. Do you see that highway?"

"Yes, sir." I was crying like a baby.

"Hit it and don't look back. This is your last chance."

I started running. I tripped on a cornstalk and fell down. My face got full of dirt. I thought, "Oh no, what's going to happen next?" I got up and started running some more. I was running, and crying, and calling out to God to please help me.

I came to the edge of the cornfield where the field met the highway. Cars were going by so fast. I thought, "Oh no, this is the world." I had forgotten what the world was like. I remembered a verse in the Bible that said His chariots would be like the whirlwind.

I stood at the edge of the road, at the edge of the world, and I said to myself, "Which way is it going to be, Marie, are you going to spend the rest of your life in an insane asylum or are you going to be free?" I looked at the highway and gritted my teeth, "I'm going to be free." I took the scarf off my head and waved it at Blackie as hard as I could.

Strange, but I felt a hand pushing on my back once I was on my way, very gently, but very firm. I put my hand back there but I couldn't feel anything. I went down the highway. Blackie had warned me to be on the lookout for the aides coming into work.

I recognized a car coming down the road and I said to myself, "Oh my gosh, here comes a car full of aides that work in the hospital." I hit the ditch and laid on my belly. I thought for a minute that by laying in a ditch I might be attracting attention so I got up. I had a great big paper napkin in my pocket. I put that up to my face and I pretended that I was having a coughing fit and kept on walking. There were five or six aides in the car; they were doing so much laughing and talking they didn't even see me.

I went into the hospital Thanksgiving Day, 1960, and I left August 20, the following year.

My trip to Minneapolis was a very, very happy one. The first ride I caught was with six young girls. They were in their second year of college. They asked me where I was going. At first I started to lie, but then I thought, "There is no sense in my lying." I didn't tell them I was running away from a mental hospital, though. I just told them I was going to Minneapolis. They asked why I was going up there when there was work in Milwaukee. I said, "I've just about worn out Milwaukee."

They were going as far as Neenah-Menasha. I knew that city because that is where they manufacture the paper towels. There is a lot of lumber and paper production there. Whoever might be interested in how paper towels are made, I recommend going there. Paper towels from tree to hanging on your rack in the kitchen. It's really something to see. Very exciting.

The girls let me out right in Neenah-Menasha. I didn't like that because inside a town or a city you really can't put your thumb out and expect to get a ride. I walked to a filling station. I needed to get a map. There was a man looking through the map rack. I asked him if there was a map of Minnesota. He pointed me to two maps of the state. I looked at the first one, but it didn't have a very good layout of Minneapolis. I looked at the other one and it had a wonderful side map of Minneapolis so I said, "This is the one I want." I made some small talk with the man at the map rack. He asked me where I was heading. I told him I was going to Minneapolis—"I have my Buick parked right around the corner." I was lying, of course; my Buick was my own two feet.

I went into the restroom at the service station and washed some of the dirt from the cornfield off my face and arms. I took my rag and wiped off my plastic bag and the cardboard box in which I had my clothes. I didn't feel afraid; I was very happy.

I was walking out of the Neenah-Menasha city limits when a car came up behind me, honking at me. I thought, "Oh boy, somebody is trying to get funny with me already." I picked up a great big rock. I was planning to put the rock right through his windshield. A man stuck his head out the window. He said, "Hey, lady, don't you remember me?" It was the man at the filling station. I laughed and said, "Oh, my goodness." He said, "Hop in, my wife and I are going about sixty-three miles and we're going west. Would that be of any interest to you?" I said, "It sure would." He said, "Put that rock down and hop in."

They took me to a turnpike and let me out. I'm not sure where I was. I wasn't afraid until I stepped off the curb. There were three roads that crossed each other and traffic was going in both directions. I got a funny feeling in the pit of my stomach. I didn't cross, but instead put my foot back on the grass. Then I went to the far side of the other road, and just as I crossed there was a big collision right where I had been standing. Three cars hit. Nobody got hurt or killed, but the cars were completely demolished, nothing left of them. That kind of took the thrill out of my trip.

I began walking down the highway backwards with my thumb out. I got several rides as the day wore on. The next ride I remember was a man about forty, not particularly handsome, but he seemed wise in the way he talked and acted. He told me he was a professor. I said, "My, my, this really is a treat." He asked why. I said, "I've never ridden in a car with a professor in my entire life. I consider this a privilege."

He said he was going to Milwaukee to deliver a speech at Marquette University. I said, "Sir, sir, you are going the wrong way! You are going west; Milwaukee is not west, it is east. Back the direction where I came from." He pulled his car over and stopped. The sun was just starting to go down in the west; fringes of yellow and orange trimmed the horizon. He was very sorry about having to let me out, but was truly grateful that I had set him straight.

If I hadn't come along he'd have been going in the wrong direction. I was glad I was able to help him. I got out and took out my ballpoint pen. Every time I got out of a car I'd mark my map. I always had my eye on Minneapolis. This time I tried to mark my map and that pen would not write. I should have prayed, but I didn't. I thought, "Oh no, I'm going to get mixed up and lost." I also had to pass water. I thought, "There is no way I can use the toilet with cars going back and forth on both sides." Finally, I couldn't hold it any longer. First my ballpoint pen wouldn't write and then I had to go to the bathroom. I looked up and there was no traffic, not a car in sight. I hit the ditch. In my rush I dropped my pen. I looked down and there it was in a puddle of urine. I needed that pen, so I picked it up and washed it off in some muddy water and wiped it off in the grass, and do you know that pen worked just perfectly!

The sun was setting, the sky was turning black. About half an hour went by and I didn't get a ride. I asked myself, "Which is it going to be, the meadow on the left or the meadow on the right?" I knew I had to sleep someplace. I was beginning to get tired. Just then a car stopped. A man and woman in the front seat asked me where I was going. "Minneapolis—I've got to find work and get started as soon as I can because I don't have much money." The woman smiled. "That's exactly where we are going. We're only thirteen miles from the state border." I rode along with them and saw a sign which read Welcome to Minnesota. I threw both arms up into the air and shouted out, "Hallelujah, praise God!"

I was free. Wisconsin couldn't touch me.

### Minneapolis

The couple left me off in Minneapolis. I got there at six-thirty in the evening. In other words, I did some fast traveling. I was extremely fortunate. I went to the YMCA; I only stayed there one night. I couldn't hack that place.

I stayed in Minneapolis a year. I would have stayed longer, but I was continually getting lost. The streets were very difficult to learn. I'd be walking down the street and read nine hundred and then I would look up and read a hundred and fifty. It was extremely confusing. There were so many one-way streets, if you'd turn off one one-way street you'd end up on another one. There was no end to it.

The outside world was too much for me. For about three weeks after arriving I was confused. I couldn't control myself, I cried a lot. Sweat poured off my body. I prayed, but it was like beating my head on a stone wall. I couldn't eat. Couldn't keep any food down. On the inside I felt like I had just jumped off a cliff.

I spent most of my time in a beautiful park. One of the things I liked about Minneapolis were the flowers. There were flowers everywhere. I loved the flowers in the park.

God sent a very kind man, I know he did. There was an old man at the park. He came over to me. He saw me sweating and shaking and crying. He said, "Lady, is there anything I can do for you?"

I answered, "No, I don't think so. I've had a nervous breakdown and I don't know if I am going to get any better or not. I have to try."

He asked, "What is it like to have a nervous breakdown?"

I said, "The suffering is more than you can possibly imagine. Worse than any physical suffering I have ever known."

He said, "I work for *Redbook,* the ladies' magazine. I write stories and take pictures. You are a very attractive woman." I didn't believe him. "Yes, you are if only you would smile. Please smile, I want to take a picture of you.

I only have two pictures of Minneapolis so far. I need something very, very unusual. You are a very unusual person. You are a very brave woman."

He told me to stand by a bunch of huge flowers, calla lilies. These calla lilies were about three feet tall, just gorgeous. Their blooms were about as big as a dinner plate and fire red.

I warned him that I didn't want any picture of my legs. I had bad legs. I walked behind the flowers. He said, "If you want to look sad it's okay. Just look how you feel." I put my hand on the blossoms and looked up at him, tipping my head. I smiled and he snapped my picture.

The kindness of this stranger struck me. I told him, "I'm stone broke. My rent's almost up and I can't pull myself together. What's going to happen to me? Am I going to die or what?"

He put his hand on my arm. "Marie, you are not going to die and you are going to get completely well. You are going to surprise your own self."

I didn't believe him. I had never been more scared in my entire life. I couldn't face life, I couldn't face the world.

He told me to walk down Hennepin, to begin looking for a job. He wanted to give me some money, but I told him no, that if he gave me money I would never break free. "I've got to do it alone."

I began walking down Hennepin. I had only walked a few steps when I saw a sign: Dishwasher Wanted. I peeked inside the restaurant—quite a few customers in there. I thought, "Gee, those plates aren't going to know if I had a nervous breakdown or not. It's a cinch; they aren't going to tell."

I wanted to go in and apply, but before I went in I prayed and asked God to help me stop shaking, crying, and sweating. I went into the place and said, "Good afternoon." The man at the cash register thought I was sweating from the heat. I was sweating from nerves. "I see you have a sign in the window about needing a dishwasher."

He said, "That's right. Have you ever washed dishes before?"

I laughed, "Yeah, lots of times."

"Do you know how to run an electric dishwasher?"

"Sir, I can run any kind of model you have."

"How soon can you start?"

I said, "I can start now if you want me to."

He clapped his hands together and said I was a godsend. He took me into the dishroom and there were probably two hundred dishes stacked clear to the ceiling. That was my medicine. I began to run the plates through the dishwasher, singing the whole time.

The boss's wife was a real sweet lady. She asked me how much money I needed to get started. I told them my room rent was up and I needed about twenty or thirty dollars or whatever they could spare. She said, "Well, you haven't earned that much yet, but I'll let you have twenty." I took the twenty dollars up to my landlady and that covered one week's rent with some left over for groceries.

At work I wore a wool skirt and it had to be over one hundred degrees in the dishroom. One day the boss's wife told me to take my break in the front where I could cool off in the air-conditioning. She tried to convince me to stop by offering me some homemade apple pie just out of the oven.

I said, "Oh boy, save me a great big piece of it." I hurried up and ran the dishes through. I worked until I got every single dish washed including the silverware. I went out front with a big white apron tied around me and relaxed. I was beginning to be Marie again.

One of Marie's idiosyncrasies was that she never wore socks under her well-worn tennis shoes. Another trademark was a big sweater that served as a winter coat. One fall, concerned about the poor health of her legs and the fast approach of winter, we got together to get her some protection. We bought her a nice warm coat with a scarf, mittens, a pair of warm wool socks, and some warm, fleece-lined winter boots. She was so thankful and seemed to walk straighter as she left pushing her cart down Malden Street.

One does not wear all of one's wardrobe every day, so well into the winter when Marie arrived in her old attire right down to bare feet in slush-soaked tennis shoes, we were alarmed. "Marie, what happened to your boots and socks?" "Well, you see, I had this friend whose shoes were worse than my tennis shoes so I gave her the boots and socks." "And the coat? Marie! Not the coat." "Well, I was walking down the street and saw a man who had nothing, just a T-shirt, so I gave him the coat and scarf. After all, I have my sweater."

—Linda Meints

## Sally Patterson

One day while working at the restaurant, I looked out the window and saw Sally Patterson. I used to live next door to her in Milwaukee. I thought, "This can't be. I'm imagining things; that can't be Sally Patterson," but I jumped up. The spoon flew out of my coffee cup and coffee went all over the counter. I ran out the door and hollered her name, "Sally! Sally!" She turned around.

She became my best friend. Her real name was Sally Rhön. Full-blooded German, she was tall, about six foot one, and very, very thin. If she hadn't been so skinny she would have been a beautiful woman. She was on the other side of the street. She turned around and looked at me. She stared in disbelief; I'll be darned. I said, "Sally, what in the world are you doing in Minneapolis?"

"Oh, Marie," she said, "it's a long story. I'm broke, out of money." I invited her to come into the restaurant and have a cup of coffee. "Oh, I'm going to need more than a cup of coffee. I haven't eaten in about two or three days."

I told the waitress to give Sally whatever she wanted and take it out of my paycheck. "This is one of my best friends. I can't turn her down when she needs me." We ate and then left for a walk. We bought a great big soda pop and walked toward the park, where she told me a story.

Sally had divorced her husband, the one I knew in Milwaukee, and moved to a small town in Wisconsin. She met a man there who had a lot of money. Lots and lots and lots of money. They married.

They lived in a small hotel by a lake. The hotel looked just like a chalet, with gingerbread shutters and lace curtains at the windows. It was very picturesque, but Sally wasn't happy there. She told her husband, "This is a beautiful small town, but I'm not happy here."

"Well," he said, "would you like to go live by my mother? My mother and my sister have a big house and also a trailer house in the back. We could live in the trailer."

Sally liked that idea. "Gee, that sounds great! I could have flowers, I could do a lot of things."

So they went to live by his mother. Sally said that when she and her husband walked in, the mother's mouth flew open and so did the daughter's. They stood there with their mouths open, gasping. When he introduced Sally he said, "This is my wife." The mother began to tremble. She put her hand on the side of the sink for support. His sister, she ran out of the room real fast. Sally thought that was very peculiar, but she couldn't put her finger on just why.

Her husband ran a tool and die factory. He banked between five and eight hundred dollars every day. There were also withdrawals. Sally kept the books balanced; she had a head for business.

One thing really bothered Sally, and that was an old trunk in the little trailer house. It was always kept locked. "What's in that trunk?" she asked.

"Just a lot of stuff you wouldn't even be interested in. There's a picture of me lying naked on a pillow—you know, a baby picture. Things like that, old girlfriends and stuff. There's nothing in there you'd want to look at."

"Well, why don't you open it up so I can see it and let me make up my own mind?" He avoided the question; he never opened the trunk when she was around.

One day curiosity got the best of Sally. First, she tried a little toy hammer. She hit that padlock with the hammer, but the little hammer broke. So then she went out to the garage and found one of those big hammers that carpenters use and tried that. The lock started to move, but it didn't come off. So she thought, "Boy, I'll fix it." She went out and got a big mallet. She stood way back and took a great big swing. She hit the ceiling light, but managed to pop the lid off.

She lifted the lid and inside was a picture of her husband laying on a pillow with no clothes on just like he'd said. He looked to be about four months old. She started going through the pictures. There was a high school graduation picture and others. The next envelope scared her half to death. It was white, and it was from the Waupun State Prison. As Sally told it, she got a sick feeling right in the pit of her stomach. She opened up the envelope and read from a document. He had been convicted for the murder of his wife.

She said, "Marie, it took me about two seconds; I didn't even bother to put the letter back. I left it right there on the table where he'd see it. I was supposed to take eight hundred dollars to the bank that day, but I took half of it to escape and left the rest on the table. I wrote him a note saying, "I'm sorry to be taking your money, but I don't have no other way to get out of here."

Sally was so scared she didn't take any of her clothes; she just started walking out of town. She was afraid to take a bus in case he tracked her down. She walked a long, long way until a woman picked her up and drove her to the bus station in the next town. She went from there straight to Minneapolis.

Sally didn't have anywhere else to go so I took her up to my room. We had a lot of fun together; a lot of funny things happened. I was told by the landlady I couldn't have extra people staying in my room. So I had to sneak Sally in.

One time the maid knocked on the door, "Miss James, would you like some fresh towels and soap?" I said, "I'll tell you what, you can skip the fresh linens, but I'll take you up on the towels and soap." I tried to act natural, but my voice came out squeaky. She became suspicious and said, "Miss James, do you feel all right?" I said, "Oh, sure, sure, I feel just fine." But she must've known that something was wrong. Sally was under the bed!

Sally and I were pretty close friends till we got into an argument one day. Sally came into my house one night with her boyfriend after I had promised the landlady that there wouldn't be any male company after ten o'clock at night. I said, "I can let you in, but your boyfriend has to go." Sally was drunk and flew into a rage. She started kicking on the door, making a terrible racket. I let her in alone. I shouldn't have done that, but it was very, very cold outside and I was worried about her.

We played a game of cards and continued to argue. First, she threw the cards down on the floor and then she threw a boiling cup of hot coffee in my face. I grabbed her and I beat the living tar out of her. The next morning when I saw her face, I cried my eyes out. I loved Sally. There was never a woman in my whole life I loved as much as I loved Sally. Her face was mottled black and blue from the beating I gave her. I would have done anything for Sally. If she needed money and all I had was a dollar, I'd take fifty cents and give her the other fifty cents. It was always like that.

Sally stole my coin collection, a coin collection which I had gotten together and was worth about eighty dollars. I had coins from several different countries. I found money from Germany issued during the Second World War. I had coins from Australia, Canada, and the United States. I had one penny which was as big as a silver dollar. She stole it all. Sally was a dope addict. I didn't know it at the time, but I never saw Sally after she took my coin collection.

### Omaha

Blackie had come to Minneapolis because I asked him to. That was a very bad mistake. I found out Blackie was a dope addict and a thief. He beat me once. No, twice. One time was real bad, I almost had to go to the hospital. He was under the influence of dope both times. When I discovered this about Blackie I panicked because I had nowhere else to go.

Blackie and I split up and I began to crack up again. It was wintertime in Minneapolis, which was just awful. I had two fairly nice jobs, but in Minneapolis they didn't want to pay you anything. Very cheap labor. I knew that I had to get rid of Blackie and I couldn't stay in Minneapolis. So I racked my brain trying to think of what to do. I called my sister, Faith, long distance to tell her what had happened. She told me to come to Omaha. I didn't have any money, but she wired me some. So I shipped my stuff C.O.D. and went to Omaha, Nebraska. I had lived in Minneapolis for almost one year.

While I was living with Faith, I had a dream about my grandmother, the one who took care of me when I lived with my foster mother and father. I remembered that she prayed for me every night. I had a dream where I saw my grandmother dead. It was true. I found out she had just died. This was my last string of hope. I sunk into a depression. One day I was upstairs and my sister came up to show me a beautiful housecoat she had bought for me. It was cotton, but it sure was pretty. It had great big flowers on it and it was pink.

Faith sat on the side of the bed talking to me. I wouldn't comb my hair, I wouldn't take a bath. I wouldn't eat, I couldn't sleep. When I did eat, the food came right back up. She asked, "Whatever's the matter, Marie?"

"Faith, I've lost my will to live. I'm thirty-six years old

and I have nothing to live for. My baby is dead. All my kids are gone. My boyfriend and I broke up, my job is gone. There's nothing left."

Then one day I went into a bar and met Kevin Gelbart. Kevin was from Michigan. He was a strange person. A small fellow, very likable, but after you got to know him there was something very, very peculiar.

Ken had a job driving trucks. One time he let me drive his semi-trailer all the way from Omaha to Iowa City. When I got to Iowa City, I went to change gears and it started grating. Kevin said, "My gosh, you're going to strip my gears and I don't have money to pay for it. They'll take it out of my paycheck." He told me to get out of the driver's seat, scoot over, and let him drive. So I did. I didn't drive anymore after that. That was my first experience driving a semi trailer.

We went to Michigan together. We drove to Ludington, his hometown. I had a funny feeling going into his parents' home. When Kevin walked in the door, his father walked out—out of the house. His mother didn't say hello. She had her back to us and just continued doing her work like nothing had happened. Kevin hadn't been home for about five or six years. That struck me as being very odd. I had the feeling Kevin wasn't really their son.

I never saw a man so starved for attention, so starved for affection. Starved for someone to talk to, starved for companionship. Kevin and I never made love. It was all a lot of petting, kissing, and hand-holding. He used to say to me, "Hold me, Marie. Just hold me." Kind of pitiful, you know?

### Going to Chicago

We were living in Muskegon, going back and forth several times between Muskegon and Ludington. At some point Kevin and I decided to go to Chicago.

Kevin didn't know beans about hitchhiking. He was acting goofy. Sticking his thumb between his legs and standing way off in the weeds instead of by the road. About fifteen, twenty, thirty cars went past; at this rate we'd never get picked up. "Oh, for the love of Mike," I yelled at him. "Kevin, you let me hitch a ride or else we're going be here forever." We'd already been there about two or three hours. I stood at the edge of the highway. I held my shopping bag in my left hand and with my right arm I pointed my thumb in the way I was going. I smiled real big.

The first car went past us; the second car stopped. I looked at Kevin out of the corner of my eye, a look that meant, "Keep your big mouth shut." When we got into the car, a woman tried to make small talk with us. She said, "Lots of times we see single men and single women on the highway, but we very seldom ever see a man and a woman together."

I said, "We're on our way to Chicago. We're going down there to look for work."

"Have you been in Chicago?"

I nodded. "Yes, my son was born at Cook County Hospital."

"My baby was born there, too." We started laughing. Before we got out of the car, she gave me a fifty dollar bill. Kevin made a grab for the money, but I got it. She let us out in Benton Harbor, Michigan.

We got into an argument outside of Benton Harbor where all the sailboats come in and out. I was furious. We got a ride and Kevin blurted out that we didn't have much money. After thirteen miles they made us get out. I yelled at him to keep his mouth shut.

"Maybe I don't want to go to Chicago anyhow."

I said, "Well, you don't have to, but that's where I'm going because I know there's plenty of work there and plenty of money."

So I went on to Chicago alone. I arrived in Chicago in 1963 or '64. Kevin and I met up again, I don't remember how. He got a job working on cars. I had a nice job packing cosmetics at Helene Curtis. I would get off work at three-thirty and had nothing else to do. So I would go and hang around the parking lot where Kevin worked. He taught me a lot about motors and how to fix things.

He said, "Marie, you're not doing nothing, hand me that ratchet wrench."

I had no idea what he was talking about. There are so many crazy tools laying on a bench. I didn't know what a rachet wrench was.

"Look, I've got this whole car apart, got half of it in my

hands, and I've gotta get up there and show you which one is a ratchet wrench?"

"Well, I guess so, because I don't know which one is a ratchet wrench."

From that moment on, Kevin began to teach me the names of the various tools. There were at least forty-five tools on his workbench. I learned the names of every one of them. Next I learned how to tape cars. This is done before the paint goes on. I think I could still tape a car in about forty-five minutes. Next I started to sand, prime, and paint cars. What fascinated me the most was the motor. The sound of a motor sets me wild. My heart just goes pitty-pat. I love motors.

I asked Kevin one day, "How does a motor work?" He lifted up the hood and spent about three hours showing me what makes a car work; the spark plugs, the pistons, the energy generated. Several times I have been able to help people who were having trouble with their cars. I can't change a tire anymore because they do not have tires and wheels like they did when I was younger. They're completely different.

### He Loved Me the Most

Though he was nice to me, Kevin was a dishonest person. He didn't care how much he hurt anyone. He just didn't care. He stole a car and took it over the state line; that involved the FBI. Kevin told them we were married. I tried to stick up for him by telling them I was his wife. The FBI followed me around and showered me with questions. Finally I left the neighborhood to get rid of the FBI.

I began getting a knowledge of city life and gaining self-confidence on my jobs. I had many, many different kinds of jobs. I hated myself because I jumped from job to job. I don't believe there are many kinds of work I haven't done except run a computer. After I started a new job I'd be very excited, but as soon as I learned everything there was to learn, I'd lose interest. I'd get a longing to go somewhere else, do something different, and meet new people.

Traveling affected me the same way. I've lived in seventeen different states and traveled my whole life. It seems no matter how much you travel, it is like a dream. No matter where you go you always say to yourself, "Gee I wonder what the people are like in Switzerland, I wonder how they live, what they eat, I wonder how they dress, I wonder what they do for fun." It is this curiosity that drove me to wander.

I went back and forth between Chicago and Omaha many times to see my sisters, Faith and Chloe. I don't know what ever happened to Kevin, but when I went back to Omaha, my oldest sister said she saw him. Kevin had married. He told her, "Oh, I wish I had Marie back. I like my wife, she's pretty good to me, but I sure did love Marie. I loved her the most."

I ended up in a rotten neighborhood of Chicago, in Uptown, over on Buena Street. I was living with an Italian man and a housekeeper. I couldn't make any friends in that neighborhood—I couldn't get a job. I was all tied up in knots; I didn't know which way to turn.

Then I wound up living down in the Loop with a girl. That didn't last either. I would hold down a job three weeks—three weeks if I was lucky. I don't remember where I went after that.

I think a woman on the street told me about day work. I was completely broke: I didn't have a penny. I had lost my nerve to go out and look for steady work at a factory. I looked bad—my clothing, my hair, everything. I went into a bar and tried to clean myself up as best I could, but I had to force myself to do it. I had lost my drive. I began working at the temporary agencies for daily pay.

⊠ ⊠ ⊠

I was working down at the agency when I met my second husband. He was a big mistake, too. I was happy for a little while. My husband was about six feet tall and extremely handsome. He was from Boston. His name was Steve Haystone. At work they called him Stosh. He had a lot of friends. My second husband and I never had sex. I take that back—we did have sex one time. It wasn't much, but I let him think it was. I believe he was a homosexual.

I know he was an alcoholic. He also took drugs of some sort, but he would never tell me what kind. He'd be gone for months and then come back. I got tired of this kind of relationship and began getting rid of his stuff stored in the apartment. One morning around three o'clock, I heard a knock on my door. I thought it was my friend Maria at the end of the hall, but then I heard a man's voice. I was afraid.

"Open up, Marie. Open up." I had a chain on the door. I cracked the door and looked out. There was Steve. I took the chain off the door and let him in. He was high on pills or dope. I don't know which. I loved him—that's the worst part about it.

He sat in the armchair. I had been working fourteen hours a day and was deathly tired. I had a full-time job by that time, a good job that paid good money. I had about four hundred dollars hidden in the apartment. He opened the dresser drawer and took out a clean pair of socks. I crawled back in bed because I was tired. He took his shoes off and changed his socks. He didn't say anything. He went to the refrigerator, but it was nearly empty. He started drinking my milk and that was all the milk I had for my cereal the next morning. I had to get up early and go to work. So I said, "Hey, wait a minute. You've been gone for five months and now you're going to come up here and tank up on my milk? No way, man."

I gave him a twenty dollar bill to go someplace and get his own groceries. He wouldn't do it. We got into an argument and he grabbed me around the throat. He bent me over backward toward the dresser. As I went back I thought, "He's going kill me for sure." On one side of the dresser I kept my hairbrush, perfume, and deodorant, and on the other side I kept my husband's stuff, his tweezers and a little pair of sharp scissors that he used to cut the hair out of his nose. I had my hands up in the air grabbing at the dresser. I thought, "I've got to get ahold of something to save my life, because if I don't I'm going to be dead," and I felt those scissors.

He had such a tight grip on my throat I was starting to black out. My tongue was hanging out of my mouth. He was squeezing harder and harder around my throat. Instead of fighting him, I concentrated on relaxing. I let my body go limp just like a dishrag. He didn't let go, but he loosened up, and that's all I needed. I raised up real quick and dug the scissors into his belly as hard as I could. I heard a sound like a tire going flat. "Pffftt," just like the air coming out of a balloon.

He went down on the floor and I thought, "I've killed him for sure." He didn't get up. I ran out of the door and into the street waving both arms until a squad car came along. I said, "Please come quick, I don't know if I've killed my husband or what. I don't care what you do with me, it doesn't matter anymore. I want you to save my husband's life."

A pile of squad cars showed up; cops were all over the place. They hauled me off to jail.

I stood in front of the district attorney. "You know Miss James, we're going throw the book at you. You're headed for state prison, there's no way you can escape it." I wanted to tell him what happened, but I kept my mouth shut because I thought, "If I sass these people, they're in a position to really fix me good."

They took me and locked me up. I went to lie on the mattress; there was a hole in it and it went "pffttt," just like my husband's lung. The following morning they took me and the other female inmates to a small cell. From there they handcuffed us together and took us to the California Street jail. I got handcuffed to a lesbian. They hooked a great big padlock on the back of the paddy wagon and took us to California Street. Then from California, I went to the Bullpen, then from the Bullpen, I went before the judge. When I got before the judge, he said, "You know that you're here on quite a serious charge. You're here for attempted murder. Did you intend to kill your husband?"

I said, "Yes, I think I did, because the only thing I could think about was saving my life." I told him my husband was near to choking me to death.

The judge looked at my husband and asked him, "Are you going to press charges?" Steve started crying, "No, she's a good wife."

The judge told me I was free to go. I went home, but after that I knew my husband and I were through. We never divorced.

### Speed Operator

During this time I had a good job. I was making about six dollars an hour working in the west part of town, out in the suburbs. I was running a punch press at high speed. Feeding the materials to the machine had to be done by hand. I'm extremely fast with my hands. When I first came in, the boss took one look at my clothes and one look at me and said, "Lady, I don't believe you can run a punch press." I said, "Why don't you try me?"

He took me to the punch press room. He said, "Do you know how to run a punch press like this?" I said, "Sir, I can run every punch press that's in this room." He said, "I'm going to show you how the pieces have to go into press." He sat down and pushed his foot on the peddle and took the piece out. "Now I want you to sit down and do it my way."

"Sir," I said, "I'm a speed operator, I can't work like this."

He said, "Well, what do you mean?"

I said, "I'm a high-speed operator. I have to have my material right up by the machine. I can run this machine blindfolded, but I have to have everything so I can touch it. I don't go by sight, I go by touch. I got to feel the die above, I've got to feel the die below, so I know exactly how everything fits."

He had never seen anyone like me. I asked, "Have you got a stopwatch?"

"Yeah. I got one right in my pocket."

"Give me a chance to get my rhythm going first, then I'll pick up speed." My hands flew over the press. I felt life rising up inside of me. I was regaining the desire to go on. It was a blessing in disguise being a speed operator.

※ ※ ※

I was working terrible, long hours, but was pulling in about four hundred a week. That was a lot of money for a girl who started out standing by a fence line feeding calves from buckets. I didn't even have a high school diploma. I ate my meals in a restaurant. I picked out anything on the menu that I wanted and ate it. I didn't care if it was shrimp or whatever. Usually it was pork chops because that's what I liked the best.

If I saw anything in the store, I just walked in and bought it. If I saw somebody on the street hurting, it was nothing to hand them a twenty or fifty dollar bill.

About this time I started feeling peculiar, like I was getting ready to faint. I had always pretty much been a well person although I had spells where everything would go black. I thought it was either my imagination or I was going through my change. My lips would go numb, then my fingertips, and my toes.

One day at work I blacked out. I woke up with my hands to my sides, and my head lying on top of my punch press. My foot was still on the pedal and the machine was going eighty miles an hour. Just think; if my head had gone into the die, it would have been completely cut off.

I went to the doctor, but I got the runaround. I should have gone to Cook County Hospital where I would have gotten help right away, but I didn't. Needless to say, I couldn't keep that job.

### I Left the Plums Behind

In the next months my whole life came to a climax. I was living about two blocks south of Evanston. People call it

Evanston, but it's really not. It's right off of Howard. I had an apartment there on Hermitage Avenue.

One day I decided to visit my old neighborhood in Uptown. I went to my favorite place to eat, the restaurant on the first floor of the Uptown Bank building. It was huge, about forty tables. I was having coffee with some old friends when who should walk in but Steve.

He walked over and said hi to me. I knew right away something was wrong. He was thin and pale. "Marie, I've got tuberculosis."

He was admitted to the city tuberculosis sanitarium out on Pulaski Road. I visited him every day just to give him moral support. His system was run-down from all the drinking. He looked like the walking dead. His cheeks were all sunken; he didn't have any meat on his arms or on his legs. Just skin and bones. His pants wouldn't stay up, he was so skinny. I felt he was at death's door.

While Steve was in the sanitarium he was either popping pills or drinking alcohol. One of his eyes went one way and the other eyeball went the other way. When he talked he didn't make any sense. "Steve," I said, "you're taking something." "Sure," he said, "I hop over the fence and there's a six-pack under a rock on the other side of the road." He did that until he climbed over the fence and broke his ankle.

I went to see him after his accident and he acted very goofy. The last time he had gone over the fence he had picked a paper sack of plums for me. He knew I dearly loved plums. I left the plums behind and never went back. Somebody told me he died out there.

❈ ❈ ❈

With time on my hands I discovered I could write. I sent a few stories to *Redbook* and some other ladie's magazines and *Reader's Digest*. One story was called "An Angel Running," which was about my foster mother running behind a lumber wagon in an old, faded dress. I got a lot of satisfaction out of writing.

Another discovery occurred at about the same time I began writing. I found out I couldn't land a job as easily as before. I was standing in line waiting to be interviewed for this job as a waitress. I was forty years old and I knew for a fact that I was a better waitress than the girls ahead of me. One was only sixteen years old. Another one was seventeen, another one eighteen, another nineteen, but they got hired. I had experience and these other girls didn't. The people hiring told me right to my face, "We don't want experienced people, we want to train the people ourselves the way we want it done." Well, that came as quite a blow to me.

I tried to get a job with the phone company, at Illinois Bell. On the written test I scored the highest. I came in with a ninety-one average. There were people there who had two or three years of college and I beat them. I couldn't believe it.

The phone company gave us a second test. They had us sit behind a huge board where we would answer the telephone, "Hello" or "Good morning." When I answered, a man asked for directory assistance. I tried to help him, but he began to curse me, calling me all kinds of rotten dirty names. I just said, "I'm sorry sir, that's what it says in the telephone book." He continued to rant and rave, but I remained calm.

A supervisor came out from behind the board and said, "Oh, Miss James, you did wonderful." I said, "What are you talking about?" He said, "That was me. Yes, we have to do that to test the girls, to find out how they are going to respond." He admired me for having that much patience with someone that was screaming and cursing. The girl next to me failed. She cursed the man back. He came around and put his hand on her shoulder and said, "I'm sorry, we can't use you."

But even though I made the highest score I didn't get the job; I couldn't pass the physical. I couldn't pass because of the veins in my legs. I cried my eyeballs out.

※ ※ ※

Things were really getting hard for me financially. I just couldn't find a way to make any money. Then one day I got a phone call and discovered I was rich.

A man on the phone said, "Marie, don't you want your money?" I said, "What money? I don't know what you're talking about."

"Well, when we hired you, we asked if you wanted to join the credit union and you said 'yeah.' We took at least a couple hundred every week out of your paycheck. We've got it for you; it's over eight thousand dollars. Do you want it?"

I said, "Oh, my gosh! I'm taking a taxicab. I'll be right up to get it."

I looked bad—unwashed, dirty, my clothes ripped. I had a hard time convincing the cab driver to wait for me. I said, "Listen, I got eight thousand dollars in there, just sit here and wait for me while I go and get my money. It might take me fifteen, twenty minutes, maybe a half-hour, but when I come out, I'll give you a twenty dollar tip." He didn't believe me; he took off.

I went in and got the money. I called for another taxi and waited forty-five minutes. I tipped the driver two hundred dollars; he almost fainted. I got home and put all that money on the table; there was over eight thousand dollars. Some of it was falling on the floor. I laid my head on my arms and cried like a baby.

Plenty of money was something I wanted all my life and now that I had it, it didn't mean anything to me. I had no one to share it with. All my riches did for me was to remind me that not one of those fifty dollar bills could put its arms around me and say, "Marie, I love you."

⊗ ⊗ ⊗

In the midst of my money windfall, I got a letter that my mother was dead. Memories flooded over my mind. I felt tired and sick; I didn't want to live without my mother.

I left my house. There was over six thousand dollars cash in my dinette drawer. I didn't even close my front door. I ran down the street toward Howard Street and up to the L-train; I was going to jump.

The whole time I waited for the L-train I was slapping my leg just like an old farmer. I said, "Come on, L-train. Come on. You can't come too fast to suit me." There was a little old man on the platform. He was running toward me yelling, "Somebody stop that woman! She's going to jump, I tell you!"

Before he got to me, I could hear my mother's voice talking to me. I began to cry. I remembered the time we were crossing San Diego Bay. We were on the deck of the boat and she said to me, "Marie, why won't you eat your cherry pie with the ice cream on top?" Nobody could make me laugh like my mother. I laughed all the way home from the L station. Walking back to my apartment I laughed like a hyena.

I went in the front room and I got on my knees and I said, "God, I am sick and tired of the kind of life that I have. My health is failing, I'm not happy. I'm at the end of my rope." I was disappointed with every love affair I had ever had because the kind of love I was looking for wasn't out there. I wanted a man that would rather die than lose me.

On my knees I told God, "God, I'm not sorry for my sins. I enjoy my men, I enjoy my liquor, I enjoy my cigarettes. I enjoy telling a little lie every now and then. I enjoy it all—I'm not gonna lie to you. So will you do me a favor? Please make me sorry for my sins." I got up from my knees. I didn't understand the prayer I was praying.

It was 1966 in August when I prayed that prayer. I didn't expect anything, not even an answer to my prayer. All my life I had prayed and never got the kind of answer I had wanted. All my life I had been tormented by memories. I just wanted it all to end.

## A River Runs Deep

At three o'clock the next day the telephone rang. "It's Ellen. Your daughter."

I hadn't seen Ellen since she was about five years old. She said, "I want to see you." After awkward small talk we decided to meet the next evening.

I was forty years old. I was tired, I was beat. I didn't know what Ellen might expect. The following night, I couldn't find anything to put on. I wore a little cotton dress and some nylons with black leather sandals. I washed and styled my hair.

I thought, "Now what does a mother take to a daughter whom she hasn't seen for almost twenty years?" I went into a store that sold expensive gifts.

"How much are your roses?" I asked.

"Ten cents apiece. Which color do you want?"

I couldn't imagine what color Ellen preferred. I guessed, "Red." I bought three dozen roses. I had a hard time carrying them.

It was not enough. Another store, "Could you suggest a good wine that would be for a reunion, two people who love each other?" The sales clerk suggested a sweet red wine.

I went out of the store loaded down. I climbed the platform to the catch the L train to the South Side. I got a terrible pain in my chest. Suddenly I was so dreadfully tired, weak; I wondered if I would make it, but I was not going to miss seeing my daughter. I got to the Loop and found that I had to walk about four blocks and then board the Illinois Central. When I got off the Illinois Central I called a cab.

I finally arrived at the address Ellen gave to me. I rapped on the door and somebody said, "Come in." Just as I turned the doorknob, the hair stood right up on my arms. I heard a voice inside my head, "You're too late, Marie, you're too late. It's all over."

But in spite of the fear I walked in . . . and stood staring. There was a young woman sitting on a sofa. My daughter was positively beautiful.

It was kind of awkward. I said, "Ellen, is that you?"

She said, "Yes, Mother, it's me."

I walked over to her and she stood to her feet. We looked at each other. I asked, "Can I hug you?" I hugged her, crying. She just stood there with her arms down at her sides, scared to death.

She said, "Do you feel bad because I didn't hug you?"

I said, "No. Why should you hug a stranger? Don't worry about it."

We sat down together on the sofa. "I gotta make sure you're my daughter. Take off your shoes, I want to see your feet."

She said, "I don't want to because there is a terrible scar on my left foot."

"Ellen, you're my girl!" I knew where she got that scar. Many years ago my husband, Ray, chased me and the girls with a piece of steel pipe. Ellen got a piece of glass in her foot, but still she ran. She was such a good little girl to run like that, she probably saved her life.

There was a sound in the next room. Ellen looked up at me, "Would you like to see your granddaughter?"

We went over to a crib and I looked down at a newborn baby. "Can I hold her?"

I looked at myself in a mirror as I held the baby. "Well, Marie, you're not sixteen anymore. You're forty years old and this is your grandchild."

I ducked my head out the window and I yelled, "I'm a grandmother! I'm a grandmother!" I thought when a person was a grandmother they would feel old, but I felt very young and youthful.

Ellen and I went into the kitchen where we talked for quite some time. "Mother, why did you give us away?"

"Ellen, I didn't give you away. I never signed any papers to give you away."

"Why didn't you come and get us?"

"I called long distance, but your foster parents wouldn't let me see you."

We talked about a number of things. Finally when I was about to leave, I remembered the gifts I had brought. I had completely forgotten about the roses and the wine.

"Oh, my gosh, Ellen, I almost forgot, this wine is for you and your husband, and the flowers are for you and the baby."

Before I left I looked at Ellen; she was so beautiful. She had everything I ever wanted. I told her, "Don't be like me, don't do what I did."

I saw her husband holding the baby and the flowers. "No matter how much you fuss and fret with each other during the day, when you go to bed at night, pull each other close and say, 'I'm sorry for the way I've been.'"

There was so much I wanted to say, but it was time to go. I had called for a cab and it was at the curb.

Ellen hugged me good-bye, "Mother, are you all right? You look so strange."

I said, "I feel strange . . . I feel something. Ellen, I feel like I'll never see you again."

"Why do you say that?" she asked.

I wasn't sure, but I thought of an illustration. "In the coal mines, it's very quiet. Sometimes underground there's a stream, very rapid and very deep. That is what I feel inside. A river just like that. Please just let me hold you one last time. Don't say good-bye. Good-byes are painful, you know? Just hold me." And she did.

I ran to my cab and jumped in. I was holding my purse and I had a shopping bag by my leg. I said, "Step on the gas as fast as you can." I had a flashback to when I left my mother standing in the middle of the street. Then I had also told the cab driver to step on it.

I looked back to see my mother one last time. I felt a rush inside of my head. "Oh, my God, I must be losing my mind. My mind is playing tricks on me. That was over twenty years ago. I'm reliving something that happened long ago."

I laughed at my own stupid mistake. I said to the cab driver, "You take your time, man, I'm just going up to the Illinois Central station." He took me there and then I went home.

⊗ ⊗ ⊗

I waited three or four days. Ellen didn't call, so finally one morning I called her. Her husband answered the telephone.

"Is Ellen there?"

He said, "Yes, Ellen's busy."

I said, "Oh. Well, can I talk to her?"

He said, "She can't talk to you right now, she's busy."

I said, "Let me tell you something, I've had six kids. No woman on earth is so busy that she can't talk to her mother. Something is wrong. I sure would like to know what it is."

He said, "Well, I'd better have Ellen talk to you then."

Ellen did come to the phone. She was crying awfully hard, and she said, "Mother, I love you, but I can't ever see you again. I can't ever hear your voice again. I just came back from the psychiatrist's office and he told me I have to stay away from you because of the memories. Mother, I'll always love you." And the telephone went click.

I couldn't believe it. I screamed, "Ellen! Ellen! My baby! My little girl!" I was screaming, but the line was dead. I panicked. How was I going to bear all this sorrow?

As I hung on to the phone I got a sharp pain in my chest. Two of them in a row. I cried, "God, help . . ." I went to take another breath to say the word "me", but I couldn't. I felt myself sinking. I knew for sure I was dying. I hung on to the telephone as I was going down to the floor and the word "me" just came out as a whisper.

I went into shock September 14, 1966.

*I keep looking for her cart in the lobby. But it is not there. No, it won't be there anymore.*

*Marie taught me to remember the important things in life. She would always inquire about my wife and children. She seemed genuinely interested, and I would share little bits about my family with her. And when we dropped her off after giving her a ride home, she would almost aways say, "Now, Chris, you be sure and give your wife and kids a hug for me," as if to say, "Oh Chris, don't ever stray away from the love they have for you. That is so important. I never really had any love like that. I want you to know how blessed you are."*

*It was her simple smile and carefree joy that cut through whatever was on my mind at the time . . . and convicted me. Here was this amazing lady. She had no family, lived in a little old run-down apartment. She pushed her cart on the streets of Uptown almost every day, in the cold and the heat. And still, here she was—smiling, happy, alive in Jesus.*

*It is probably going to take me a while to stop looking for her cart. It is still hard to believe she's gone from us. But I do feel God's peace when I think of her death. Her suffering is done. She is at home with Jesus. And I can't wait to see her there . . . and give her a big hug.*

— Chris Ramsey

# *Shock*

When I first went into shock I thought I was having a spell with my heart. I had these sharp pains in my chest. I tried to breathe but I couldn't. It hurt too bad. Then I began to go numb all over. First my lips, my fingertips, and my toes, then my whole body went numb. I no longer had any contact with this world. None. None at all.

It was like I was riding in an airplane and the wheels of the airplane lost contact with the ground. I was aloft, gone into another world.

Pictures start coming at me, one right after another. They are in color: I see this river and a man's face floating above the water. It is a real strong river. The waves, I can see waves on the river. I can see his black hair. It is Davis. I see ice but the ice isn't clear, it is red—red with blood.

I see my body in motion. I am a small child. I am walking in a fog. I am crying, groping through the haze. And I see a barrier, it is a picket fence . . . the same picket fence that has haunted me most of my life. On the other side there is a car with a star on the side.

I hear shouting and the sound of a gun blast. It is dark and the wind is making terrible noises. Terrible, terrible noises. And the gate keeps slamming in the wind. "Davis, where are you? Where have you gone?" I am so scared. Davis is on the other side of the fence and he won't let me out the gate. Tears stain my little red sweater. I brush my hair away from my eyes.

The gate bangs open. I am lying on a body. It is Davis. My hands are sticky and wet; it feels like Karo syrup. I put my two hands together; they are red with mud. It is dirt mixed with blood. I wipe my hands on my heart where I carry all my hurt, trying to rid myself of the blood. I am covered with Davis's blood. Oh God, it is awful.

I knew I was coming out of shock when I realized I was breathing. It was terrible. I cried, "My God, oh my God, I'm in a world I don't want to be in. I don't want to live in this world."

I panicked. Who was I? Was I a little four-year-old girl? I went and looked in the mirror and I saw an old woman. Her hair was white, tangled in knots. Her face was dirty. I said, "That's me! I'm an old woman, forty years old. But how can that be? I'm a little four-year-old-girl. How in the world could I be both?

I went outside and I saw cars going by real fast. I screamed, "Oh my gosh! I'm not in the Sand Hills. This is not Davis's house. I'm in Chicago!"

I vaguely remember going to the corner grocery store for some milk. After entering the store, I sat down on a sack of potatoes. I laid my arms on the grocery counter and cried like a baby. I cried like that for about one hour. People were watching me. The man that ran the store was watching me. He just shrugged his shoulders and kept waiting on customers. After a while, I got up and walked home, like it was something people do every day of the week. A woman told me all this later.

Coming out of shock was like living in the pits of hell. I lay on the rug and pulled my hair. I kept saying, "God, I don't understand what's going on inside my head. I don't understand. I'm going crazy. Kill me now, because I don't want to live." Finally I got on my knees and started praying. I was praying so loud I bet the neighbors heard me. I began to scream, "Would you help me? Why won't you help me? "

I sat down on the sofa and I could not comprehend this sweet feeling that started to come over me, a very peaceful feeling. Like a hot summer afternoon with a nice cool breeze, that was the feeling that came over me. Then while I was sitting there smoking a cigarette I saw a vision of Jesus. I had a vision of Jesus holding me in His arms, singing to me. He told me how much He loved me.

Now, all my life the most beautiful memory I had, the sweetest memory, was my mother holding me. In the rocker, she would sit holding me close, singing and stroking my hair. I remember her telling me how much she loved me. And here was Jesus holding me, comforting me.

He was standing on the Sea of Galilee. He put His finger to His lips as if to hush a baby, "Peace." There was a terrible, terrible storm, the sky was black, and the waves were coming up high. The wind was blowing something fierce, lashing Jesus' robes around His legs. He put His fingers to His lips again as if to quiet the wind, "Peace." Everything was still and calm. I knew Jesus didn't want me screaming, but how could I go on living? How?

Then I saw myself in a peculiar-looking town with narrow streets and houses made out of stone. I went inside one of the houses; I was with someone I had known for a long time. This person was a man. He was wearing sandals of some sort and long clothes, robes wrapped around him. This man was someone I was familiar with, someone I loved.

"Are you going for a walk?" I asked.

"Yes."

"Can I come with you?"

"Yes, I'd like that very much."

"Gee, that's great. I hope it's nice outside; we'll go for a nice walk." It was so real.

We began walking and came to the edge of town. There was a hill. I looked up and saw three crosses. One big one and two small ones. This friend of mine said to me, "Marie, do you know the name of this hill?"

I recognized the place. I didn't want to go up that hill. I

looked down at the ground, almost ashamed. "Yes. It is called the hill of Golgotha."

We walked a little further. I hesitated. I really didn't want to go on. My friend asked me, "Do you want to feel bad for the rest of your life about that blood?"

"No."

He motioned to me to follow. "If you want to be free then you have to come with me. That is the only way you'll ever be free."

Jesus and I climbed the hill, but I couldn't shake my sense of guilt and shame. If it wasn't for me and people like me, full of sin, Jesus wouldn't have had to die the way he did. When we got almost to the top of the hill we stopped. I said, "I thought you said we were going to the top of the hill?"

He said, "Marie, you have to go the rest of the way alone."

I cried. I didn't like what was happening. But I walked the rest of the way alone. I looked down and there was a pool of blood about the size of a turkey platter. It kept going drip, drip, drip, and I looked to see where the blood was coming from. It was coming from my friend, from His side. There was a spear stuck in there. Stuck in so far that it stuck to the wood on the other side. Drip, drip, drip. I looked at my friend's face and all I could see was love. Love was the only thing I could see, the only thing I could feel, and I knew it was Jesus.

The pain, the pain.

God revealed it to me. God showed me that Jesus didn't die from the spear wound, but from a broken heart. He had the sins of the whole world on His breast. It was more than He could bear because while He was dying He called out, "My God, my God, why have you forsaken me?" Jesus was all alone, all alone, He had no one.

As I transferred my love from Davis to Jesus, the Son of God, I realized how much Jesus loved me. I wasn't saved yet but I was going through the process of being saved. I realized it was Jesus' love I had been looking for—that no man could satisfy.

Davis said over and over that he loved me. With Davis was the only time I felt like someone special—that I was loved. But, as I got older, mixed in there was a confusion. He couldn't have loved me. I cannot think of anything lower than for a man to molest a child. A little child is old enough to understand some things but they cannot apprehend them completely. I was innocent. I was only four years old. I only knew that I felt loved. But Davis's love was not a good love; he was rotten to the core. I can't think of anything worse a man could do. Being sexually molested by the only person I thought loved me was the pain I carried all my life.

Jesus must have understood how I felt—never having a home, growing up in the orphanage, living with my foster mother, running away from Ray. He knew me when I was happy in California, when I waded into the ocean. He loved me when I lost my children, both times. He was with me in the state mental hospital. I was never alone.

I told a brother at the front desk at Jesus People, "I know God and Jesus love me." He said, "Oh, Jesus loves everybody." I said, "Yeah brother, but you don't understand. You don't know how much. That's the part that you don't understand."

That's the part that I want to tell everybody. If they knew how much Jesus cared! Do you think God wanted that to happen to me? Or Jesus wanted me to suffer like that? *No way! No way!* God or Jesus doesn't want anybody to suffer the way that I suffered. Suffering does not come from God. God loves His people too much.

After working through the feelings I was happy. When I walked down the sidewalk it was like I was walking on air. I felt like I was half drunk. That sore that ate at me day and night, it was gone. And in its place there were little tinkle bells. Those little bells would tinkle every place I went. God is forming something on the inside of us; knowing this helped me.

This is a very important part of my story. As a child I couldn't understand, as a teenager I couldn't understand, as a young married woman I couldn't understand. I still can't understand how God works, but this I know: that everything that hurt me and confused me played a very important part in what brought things together for me to find God. Just like a puzzle it finally came together.

It's all I can do to sit here quietly and talk to you with this tape. It's all I can do to sit in this chair. I want to go up Broadway and Wilson and shout, "I'm rid of my misery forever! Jesus took it all away from me!" I want to go down to State and Randolph, I want to shout, "Jesus took my misery away from me! Jesus took all my agony away!" I want to get on a TV station. I want to stand on the top of the whole world and tell what Jesus did for me.

*What happens to a child when a grownup who gains the child's trust and love sexually uses that boy or girl for his own gratification? What does or can that kind of inner conflict do to the mind and spirit and soul of that child? Marie is one tragic answer to those questions.*

*There were vivid Christ symbols in Marie's story of Davis: he was the savior for the lost little girl, making her feel worthy and loved, creating for her a sense of redemption. In her shock experience she imagined Davis dying for her, she saw Marie, the child, wiping his shed blood over her heart. Yet the fatal dagger was the truth that Davis, of all the people in her life, ravished not only her body, but also her innocence, her wellness of mind, and her ability to trust. As Marie disclosed "being sexually molested by the only person I thought loved me was the pain I carried all my life." Yet in the midst of the images of a false christ, of a betrayer came the true healer, the true lover— the Restorer.*

—the editors

# *Afterword*

Marie spent the next thirty years living in Chicago transient hotels and single-room apartments. She became identified as a bag lady—an unkept woman pushing her loaded cart around the city. To most she remained anonymous, but to the Jesus People she became a friend.

Marie first visited the mission in 1981. Her habit was to come around for a few months and then drop out of sight for as many more months. Her patterns and behavior were unpredictable. At one point she was invited to move in and live with us, if only she would get rid of her cats and quit smoking. Of course, she would also be required to take baths and keep her room tidy. Marie flatly refused.

At the Jesus People dinner guest program and several other centers, Marie became a fixture, playing her piano, smiling, and talking to everyone she met. She bombarded unsuspecting guests with her stories, often calling across the lobby, "Brother, Brother, Sister, Sister" and then launching into a fragment of the puzzle. The bewildered "brother" and "sister" might sit for a minute hearing a tale of escaping from a mental institution or of the FBI chasing her. They probably thought she was mad.

Over my five months of taping Marie's story a change took place in my perception. Marie, with her ragged clothes and cigarette-stained teeth, became less pathetic and more human. Something happened inside of me. I was profoundly touched by her story. I came to know her as more than a bag lady, as a friend.

Marie died in March of 1996; she would have been seventy years old. At her second-to-last taping session, as we were finishing up, Marie said, "You know, Jane, I am going to die." "When, Marie?" I asked. "Soon," was all she said. By mid-March she had missed two taping sessions so I asked a "brother" to go to Marie's apartment to check on her.

"You know Marie comes and goes," he said.

"I know, but this time it's different. She knew she was dying."

Joe and Chris went to her apartment. They knocked at the door but got no answer. Finally, Joe climbed out on the fire escape and looked in the dirty window. He saw a flame lit on the stove and cats crawling over trash stacked three feet high. The police came and got the landlord to let them in. They found Marie lying dead on the bathroom floor. The Cook County coroner's report said it was a heart attack. She had been lying there for three days.

Marie's body went to the county morgue until next of

kin could be notified. After three months a relative was not found and she was buried at the county's expense in a pauper's grave.

At her memorial service many people from all walks of life came together to mourn Marie's passing and to share how she had touched their lives. The room was full of human service professionals, transients, soup kitchen volunteers, shelter residents, and shelter providers; we all had a story to tell.

⌖ ⌖ ⌖

After working on Marie's story for a year, shaping the transcripts and checking high school and medical records available to me, I thought I had come to the end. A phone call brought final closure.

Bertie McBride, my research aide in Belgrade, Nebraska, called. "Sorry it has taken me so long to get back to you. There has been so much snow and the courthouse was closed for Arbor Day. Well, anyway, it looks like we have found your Davis. He was a stepbrother to Marie's mother, the son of Tillie from a previous marriage. Tillie was the second wife of Marie's grandfather, 'the one who ran the Loretta Hotel.'"

I was relieved to have this one last loose thread wrapped up. "Great. When did he die?"

"He died a natural death up in Washington state. Apparently, the state of Nebraska brought charges against him, but I wasn't able to verify the case because all the court documents have been destroyed. Oh, no, he wasn't killed; he left the state and ended up in Idaho and then Washington."

⊠ ⊠ ⊠

Marie James was a bag lady. She was not of noble birth, she was foolish and weak, rejected by society, abused, and neglected. She kept cats in trash-filled apartments. She drank sour milk, ate stale bread, and manufactured her own cigarettes from butts she found on sidewalks. Marie smelled bad. She wore men's clothing—ragged, worn, and dirty. To me she was beautiful, wise, and strong. I miss her so much.

> God chose what is foolish in the world to shame the wise,
> God chose the weak in the world to shame the strong,
> God chose what is low and despised in the world, even
> things that are not, to bring to nothing things that are.
>
> 1 Corinthians 1:27, 28 RSV